War & Peace

IN THE WORKPLACE

Other titles by Jeanne Martinson

Lies and Fairy Tales That Deny Women Happiness

Escape From Oz – Leadership for the 21st Century

Available at www.martrain.org

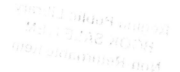

War & Peace

IN THE WORKPLACE

DIVERSITY
CONFLICT
UNDERSTANDING
RECONCILIATION

A non-fiction book by
Jeanne Martinson

Distributed by:

Martrain Corporation and Personal Development
P.O. Box 1216
Regina, Saskatchewan
Canada S4P 3B4
www.martrain.org
Tel: 306.569.0388
Fax: 306.569.0302

Cover art by Susan Penner, Designs for You by Susan.

Library and Archives Canada Cataloguing in Publication

Martinson, Jeanne, 1962–

War and Peace in the Workplace: diversity, conflict, understanding, reconciliation/Jeanne Martinson.

Includes bibliographical references and index.

ISBN 0-9685370-2-2

1. Diversity in the workplace. 2. Conflict management. I. Title.

HD42.M37 2005   658.3'008

C2005-905558-8

DEDICATION

To my father,

Marlin C. Martinson
1923 — 2003

*He taught me
to appreciate Canada,
travel the world
and come back grateful.*

Acknowledgements

Many people have shared their knowledge and caring with me and I thank them for their openness and involvement, particularly:

My clients and workshop participants for sharing their diversity issues and challenges with me.

My editorial review team–Alda Bouvier, Malcolm Bucholtz, Pat Dell, Fran Donaldson, Donalda Ford, Christina Kaya, Darci Lang, Laurelie Martinson, Velma Martinson, Tracy Meyers, Pauline Relkey, Carolyn Schur, Carole Stepenoff, Jim Roscoe and Kathleen Thompson–for donating their time, patience and energy to review the manuscript and offer suggestions and comments. This book is much improved due to your talents.

My friends and family for supporting me emotionally through this year of chaos, especially my husband, Malcolm.

My research assistant, Taryn Bemister for her many hours in libraries and for making my research piles disappear into neat labeled files.

My graphic artist, Susan Penner for her fabulous cover design and book formatting.

To all of you, thank you.

(*Acknowledgement: Ack!* Those who *know* my work and have stood out on the *ledge* with *me*.)

NOTE FROM THE AUTHOR

This book could have been 500 pages if I had explored every kind of diversity in Canadian society today. But surveys show few people buy books 500 pages long unless the main character is Harry Potter.

No doubt there will be those who feel that areas that were not covered should have been. No doubt others feel certain topics and issues were chewed on far too long. Either way, I endeavored to bring you a new and innovative way of looking at diversity in the workplace.

Thank you for purchasing this book. But more importantly, thank you for considering looking at yourself and your workplace with new eyes.

Jeanne Martinson

TABLE OF CONTENTS

CHAPTER ONE
We Can't Ignore Diversity

Each summer, a tour group of approximately 75 international high school students travel across Canada. They are Rotary Exchange Students and represent over 40 different countries[1] – from Brazil to Bangladesh. As a Rotarian, I am involved with hosting the group for the one evening while they are in Regina. During one of these tours, I asked a girl from Denmark if she experienced conflict while spending time with people from such different cultures. "Absolutely," she said. "When it happens, we just throw up our arms, say, "It's cultural" and walk away."

Whether we are students or employees, we may spend a major part of our day with people we would not socialize with outside of the workplace. We just don't seem to have much in common and those differences often create conflict. For the students on the bus tour, having the option of walking away is a good one. But this option is hardly realistic in the workplace where we may be working cubicle to cubicle with the person we are experiencing conflict with.

While diversity can be problematic and can trigger conflict, toxic work groups, low morale, harassment, misunderstandings and employee turnover, it can also be wonderful. It can create benefits for individuals and organizations when diverse perspectives are utilized to create synergy to move an organization forward.

Many organizations have adopted a respectful workplace or harassment policy to combat the challenges of a diverse workplace. But this isn't enough to minimize diversity-based conflict or to realize the benefits of a diverse workforce. We need to shift how we perceive and work with others.

The diagram below illustrates the choice we have to make regarding diversity in our workplace. Diversity creates conflict. Once conflict exists, do we allow our relationships to spiral down into dysfunction? Or do we become aware of how we perceive the world, understand the differences between ourselves and others, and work towards reconciliation?

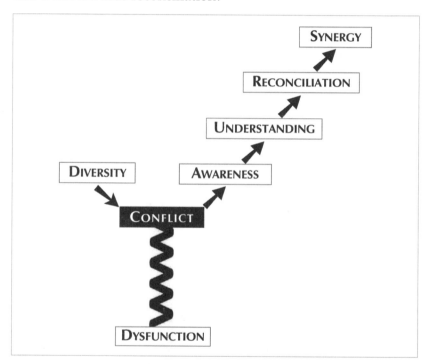

This book is titled *War and Peace in the Workplace* because many of the workplaces I see in client organizations are described by employees as war zones and their workmates as either enemies or allies. Many of our workplace conflicts can be traced to our diversity – both our diversity in the big 'D' issues such as race, gender, or ability but also diversity in the small 'd' issues such as values, marital and family status, age or thought processing.

The symbol at the beginning of each chapter resembles a globe in an oyster shell. Our workplace is becoming more diversified as the world becomes smaller. We do business across the globe when we used to do business down the street. We have immigrants coming from every continent on the planet with their own religious beliefs, cultural norms, languages and way of being.

As an example of our world becoming smaller, consider that Toronto, Canada's largest city is considered to be the most diverse major city in the world, with 175 different countries of origin represented.[2] According to Randy McLean, Manager of Economic Policy for the City of Toronto, of the 2.5 million people who live in Toronto, 45% are visible minorities and 50% of that group are born outside of Canada. Understanding and managing diversity is vital for Toronto and is a growing priority across the country.

Like the oyster pearl, we are many layered. We are different from our co-workers in many ways and all of these diverse layers can create conflict if we are not conscious of how we think about ourselves and others.

No one wants a workplace that feels like a refugee camp where the future is uncertain and day-to-day life carries a world-weary hopelessness. We have choices as to whether our workplaces are war zones or enriching environments. We have more control than we realize to avoid dysfunction and move through awareness, understanding, and reconciliation to synergy.

ENDNOTES

1. Rotary International Student Exchange program is a year-long exchange for grade 11 and 12 students between two countries where Rotary Clubs are willing and able to host. The students attend school and cultural events in their host country while acting as ambassadors for their home country. The goal of this program is to work towards world peace and understanding.

2. Randy McLean in telephone interview July 2005.

CHAPTER TWO
What Is Diversity Anyway?

'Diversity' is a word that is tossed around in many areas of work and social life, and has come to mean different things to different people. To a stockbroker, it means a balanced portfolio of stocks, bonds and other investments. To a horticulturalist, it means balancing perennials, annuals, shade and sun. In the workplace, it means any point of human difference.

How we define it personally or how the term is used in our workplace is important to consider and clarify so that discussions around the issue are based on common understanding.

Diversity can be defined by the four employment equity categories of: visible minorities; women in non-traditional or management roles; persons with disabilities; and aboriginal persons.[1]

Diversity could likewise be defined by what is termed the protected or prohibited grounds in Canadian and provincial Human Rights legislation. These categories include race or colour, religion or creed, sex (including pregnancy), sexual orientation, marital status, family status, physical or mental disability, national or ethnic origin, ancestry or place of birth, age, dependence on drugs or alcohol, and source of income.[2]

Diversity could also be defined by provincial or federal labour law to include race, creed, religion, colour, sex, sexual orientation, nationality, ancestry, place of origin, marital status, family status, disability, physical size or weight – which is a slightly different list from the two above.3

For the purposes of the discussions in this book, consider diversity to be the recognition of the large and small ways that people are different.

The smallest difference can create workplace conflict; the smallest difference can also challenge our 'groupthink'4 and create synergy. Until we respect and value each others' differences this synergy is not available to us.

While on a recent trip to northern Ontario, my husband Malcolm and I completed 30 crossword puzzles.5 I would work them as far as I could and then pass them over to him. He would complete the words he knew, using my words to trigger his vocabulary and memory. I would then use his words to trigger my own. Between the two of us, we usually finished a puzzle. If we worked singularly with the scope of only our own language and ability, completing any of the puzzles would seem impossible. We needed each other's diverse abilities to be successful.

In the workplace, we don't often value ideas that are not ours. We don't value words that we did not write, solutions we did not invent. Have you ever resented solutions that were not yours or discounted words you did not write?

A key to understanding each other is to see that everyone is different. Not only are people different from me, but I am different from them. This distinction is important because the more we identify ourselves as members of the dominant group, the more we see ourselves as the norm and others as 'different'.

We may believe that change is needed on the part of 'others' so they can 'fit in', or in some cases, become more like 'us'. We are often not willing to think that our way of seeing the world is not always the correct one – that there can be other ways of thinking, doing and being.

The symbol beside the chapter title is a globe within an oyster shell. Over time, an oyster grows one of the most valued gems in society by covering a grain of sand with concentric circles of nacre. Once we start to fully utilize the diversity within our teams and workplaces (the large and small ways that people are different), our outputs will become more valuable – much like the fine pearls that an oyster produces.

ENDNOTES

1. Employment equity is a term that was coined by Judge Abella in the Royal Commission on Equality in 1984. The Royal Commission found that four categories of people were under-represented or underemployed in the Canadian workforce. They were aboriginal persons (Inuit, First Nations and Metis), women in non-traditional or management roles, persons of visible minority and persons with disabilities.

2. Organizations are federally or provincially regulated and their level of regulation determines whether they fall under federal or provincial labour law and human rights legislation. There is a slight difference between the protected or prohibited grounds list from province to province.

3. These lists are different because human rights legislation covers more than employees. Areas such as dependence on alcohol or drugs and source of income tie more directly to possible discrimination of education, services or accommodation.

4. Groupthink is a concept identified by Irving Janis (Decision making: A psychological analysis of conflict, choice, and commitment, 1977) that refers to faulty decision making in a group. Groups experiencing groupthink do not consider all alternatives and they desire unanimity at the expense of quality decisions. Groupthink occurs when groups are highly cohesive and when they are under considerable pressure to make a quality decision. Negative outcomes of groupthink include: examining few alternatives, not being critical of each other's ideas, selecting data from only selective sources, excessive stereotyping of rivals outside the group, and pressuring anyone in the group who express arguments against the group's stereotypes, illusions, or commitments, viewing such opposition as disloyalty.

5. Yes, I am aware that this could be considered an addiction.

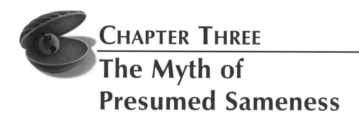

Chapter Three
The Myth of Presumed Sameness

"I am the Guardian of the Gates, and since you demand to see the Great Oz I must take you to his palace. But first you must put on the spectacles."

"Why?" asked Dorothy.

"Because if you did not wear spectacles the brightness and glory of the Emerald City would blind you. Even those who live in the City must wear spectacles night and day. They are all locked on, for Oz so ordered it when the City was first built, and I have the only key that will unlock them."

He opened the big box and Dorothy saw that it was filled with spectacles of every size and shape. All of them had green glass in them. The Guardian of the gates found a pair that would just fit Dorothy and put them over her eyes. There were two golden bands fastened to them that passed around the back of her head where they were locked together. When they were on, Dorothy could not take them off had she wished, but of course she did not want to be blinded by the glare of the Emerald City so she said nothing.[1]

To the characters in the book the *The Wonderful Wizard of Oz*, the Land of Oz truly looked green because the spectacles made it so. Everyone who entered or lived in the Emerald City saw their experience through the green glass spectacles and therefore experienced the same reality. The green view of the world became their comfort zone and the cultural norm. The visiting Dorothy and her band of merry adventurers[2] were given the key to experience the Emerald City in the same light as those who were already there.

What if Dorothy had entered the city without the glasses? She might have asked "Why does everyone think it is green here? Why is green better? Is green the only choice? Who decided that it should be green?"

The Wizard of Oz explained how he created the belief system for the occupants of Oz:

"One day, I went up in a balloon and the ropes got twisted, so that I couldn't come down again. It went way up above the clouds, so far that a current of air struck it and carried it many, many miles away. On the morning of the second day I awoke and found the balloon floating over a strange and beautiful country. I found myself in the midst of a strange people who seeing me come from the clouds, thought I was a great Wizard. I ordered them to build this City, and my palace and they did it all willingly and well. Then I thought, as the country was so green and beautiful, I would call it the Emerald City, and to make the name fit better I put green spectacles on all the people so that everything they saw was green."

"But isn't everything here green?" asked Dorothy.

"No more than in any other city," replied Oz; "but when you wear green spectacles, why of course everything you see looks green to you. My people have worn green glasses on their eyes so long that most of them think it really is an Emerald City."[3]

The more different our spectacles are from the colour of those who surround us, particularly spectacles of the dominant group, the more unwelcome and excluded we feel. This discomfort is compounded by the degree that those around us see their spectacle colour as being true and best and minimize the validity of those wearing purple peepers, blue binoculars, or salmon sunglasses.

For example, when I visited Hong Kong, I felt that I definitely had the wrong spectacles on. From the time we landed on the tiny island of Lantau that housed the international airport, I was aware of my being an outsider. The food was different as well as how you ate it. The language sounded different; the written letters impossible for me to guess the meaning. I had not received a pair of green spectacles to make the world around me make sense. I was completely amazed and confused, with no instructions.

Diversity in Canada isn't just about new immigrants to Canada. The assumptions of who a Canadian is, how a Canadian should act, and how a Canadian should think, is part of our spectacled reality. Many Canadians think that we are basically the same, with a few differences, that we have a 'Canadian' culture, and to a degree that is so. But when we think that everyone who is outside our dominant cultural norm is incorrect and needs to change, adjust or 'get with the program', we throw away the best of what Canada is and what it can be.

Culture is a general term sociologists, anthropologists and others use to refer to the whole collection of 'agreements' that the members of a particular society share. It includes all the shared points of view that define what is true, what is good and what kinds of behaviour are to be expected and tolerated. In large part, culture includes those ways of thinking, feeling and acting that the members of one society simply take for granted, but which might seem very strange to an outsider. Our culture becomes the 'proper' way of doing things.

We have a series of agreements in our larger societal culture, such as saying "how are you?" when we don't care, settling disagreements without physical violence, queuing up in lines, shaking hands and offering eye contact. All these make up our culture and are so inbred that we don't think about them not being 'right' or 'proper'. There are no obvious reasons for these agreements in our culture – any more than there were obvious reasons to put on the green spectacles in Oz. Consider the question, "Why do men wear ties?" It is a real agreement, because we negatively judge a man who couldn't be 'bothered' to put on a tie for a formal event. As new employees join a workplace culture, they don't ask the questions that illustrate our agreements. But they do know that until they accept the workplace agreements or culture, they will not fit in and therefore will not be accepted and valued.

Our beliefs and values create our agreements. Beliefs are perspectives of what is right and true. Values are perspectives of what is good and better.

An example of a widely shared belief is that God exists. It is also a widely shared view that God doesn't exist. Some people have agreed to beliefs that directly contradict the beliefs others have agreed to. If you want to fit into the workplace around you, you need to understand what the beliefs are that are in agreement. If your beliefs are too different from the beliefs of those around you, you don't have agreement and therefore your beliefs appear too alien to those with whom you are working and they see you as an outsider.

Only a small amount of our knowledge of the world originates with our personal experience. The greater part of our belief system is socially derived, handed down to us by our parents, grandparents and teachers.

Even though we may think that our beliefs are true and real, we recognize that in history some belief 'agreements' made by the dominant group of the time were later seen to be false. Centuries ago, people observed that the earth appeared to end at the horizon. Not surprisingly they concluded that if they reached the end of the earth they would drop off into nothingness. Generation after generation of children were taught the dangers of venturing out to sea, and they believed that what they were taught was correct. What we have learned from this is that beliefs can be overturned and replaced. It can be difficult, however, to regard our own personal beliefs as simply agreements and as a result, we teach the next generation our agreements as hard, cold facts.

Values are points of view about what is good. People have many agreements about values – which time system is good, which clothing style is good, what is beautiful, which style of leadership is good.

Our values determine what is better. Some people feel it is better to permit people to achieve the fullest extent of their potential even though inequalities are inevitably created in the process. Other people prefer that everyone have all the necessities of life rather than allowing some people to accumulate more than they need. Capitalists and socialists hold these two different values. Capitalists generally agree that achievement is more important than equality and socialists generally agree that it should be the other way around.

Peace is based on an agreement that no one wins if people kill each other. Others believe in an agreement that it's okay to kill in order to get what you want. You can't have a war unless both sides agree to this, even if one side feels that it's only permissible to kill to obtain peace. In the workplace our agreements about how we handle conflict can make our workplace seem like a battlefield. Our personal beliefs about aggression, assertiveness and passive behaviour when faced with conflict, can help or hinder our productivity and career success.

Values are no casual matter. Conflict often occurs in the workplace because others interpret and judge our values based on our behaviour. We believe our personal way, our department's way, our team's way is best or better and therefore see other routes to completion as inferior and judge the travelers on that alternative route harshly. An example of this could be how we see time – we might be an early bird working with a night owl. The other person's time system is different, and we see their arriving late and working late as bad. Therefore we judge the night owl as being lazy, unproductive or uncommitted.

Values are statements that some things are better than others. People can be brutal to each other when they disagree over something they value. This is partly because we tend to believe that the things we think are good are really good. If you feel peace is better than war, you probably don't regard this as a simple matter of personal preference. You feel that peace really is better and you probably have hundreds of reasons to back up your point of view. We don't leave our personal values at the door of our office, we bring them in with us. Everything we value personally can impact our workplace relationships.

If our differences mean that we fall outside of the cultural norm of the workplace, we feel excluded and not valued. In the following chapters we will discuss the agreements we have made regarding what is best and good, what is truth in our culture and

13

how that affects our workplace. We will see how our workplace is becoming more diverse and how we can move past merely understanding diversity, to utilizing and embracing differences in order to maximize our personal and corporate success.

In the business world where we have been motivated to maximize the common thought and goal, our differences get short shrift and the dominant group norm rises to the top. As long as we perceive our green spectacles are best and our workplace as truly green, we cannot move forward. We must be willing to become aware of who we are and who we are working with, understand our differences and our potential for conflict, work towards reconciliation with the goal of a synergistic work environment.

ENDNOTES

1. If you are thinking that this quote doesn't align with your recollection of the movie shown on television in December of each year, you are correct. The quotes in this chapter are directly from the book *The Wonderful Wizard of Oz*, which is dramatically different from the movie, *The Wizard of Oz*. *The Wonderful Wizard of Oz*, L. Frank Baum and W.W. Denslow, 1899.

2. Dorothy traveled with a lion, scarecrow, a tin man and her dog, Toto.

3. *The Wonderful Wizard of Oz*, L. Frank Baum and W.W. Denslow, 1899.

CHAPTER FOUR
Us and Them and We

We and They
Father, Mother, and Me
Sister and Auntie say
All the people like us are We
And every one else is They.

All good people agree,
And all good people say,
All nice people, like Us, are We
And every one else is They.

Rudyard Kipling[1]

Kipling's poem illustrates our ability to see ourselves as different from others. And more importantly, it illustrates that we see others as different from ourselves. To understand how we create this awareness of difference, we need to ask ourselves how we think and develop our beliefs and stereotypes.

When we experience life – a conversation in which we are engaged, a scene we witness, a song on the radio – we take in information about the experience through our five senses (visual, auditory, kinesthetic, olfactory and gustatory).[2] This information is molded by our mind as we delete information, focus in on other data, distort the information according to our beliefs and values, and generalize so it makes sense to us.

When taking in information, very few people stop to ask themselves, "I wonder what that meant?" We usually instantly react, without realizing that our reaction is based on our mental programming and that we are functioning in a habitual, unconscious way.

We delete information that does not agree with our current belief system and focus in on information that agrees with our beliefs. Like a front door with a sliding window insert to let in fresh air, when the information coming through builds and strengthens our belief, our mind lets it in. When the data disagrees with a belief we hold, we discount, disagree or disbelieve its validity – basically slamming the window shut.

I once had the pleasure of working with an interesting First Nations woman who was both a successful entrepreneur and a great inspiration. When describing this woman to a colleague of mine, my colleague found it hard to believe that this woman was both successful and aboriginal. With every new piece of evidence I put in front of her, she disagreed or suggested my information must be incorrect. At the end of our discussion, she amended her judgment to suggest that if this woman was actually successful, then it was "probably because she was raised in a white home and was able to rise above her heritage". She clearly had limiting beliefs about people of First Nations.

My mother is an unrelenting Blue Jays fan. If I point out a recent loss, challenging her belief that they are the greatest team on the planet, she finds a reason or excuse to defend her belief. It might be that they currently are having coaching issues or struggling with a tight playing schedule that is causing lack of sleep and poor performance. Even the weather under the covered Toronto Sky Dome has been used for justification.

The point with both of these examples is that we will go to great effort to defend the beliefs we hold. We will use excuses, arguments, alternative data, even violence. It takes a strong person to say to herself or himself, "That doesn't agree with what I know or believe. Could I be wrong? Should I investigate further?"

When we have evidence that aligns with our belief, we let it in through the screen on the door and respond to ourselves or others by saying, "See, just as I expected." We are constantly having our beliefs reaffirmed by our own selective focusing. And as we age, without questioning ourselves or becoming aware of our capacity to delete some data and focus in on other data, we become more of who we already are.

Our minds are fluid and we distort information. *In a moment, I am going to ask you not to think. Do not think of a tree with a huge trunk with rough brown bark. And whatever you do, do not put shiny green leaves on the tree or juicy red apples. Especially not the kind of apple that squirts juice on your face when you bite into it. Don't think about trees. Don't think about shiny green leaves that rustle in the breeze. Don't think about apples.*

When I use this exercise in my diversity workshops, some people have the ability to see the tree and quickly change it or block the tree by sheer will, but those who are more visual or who were not trying as hard were more susceptible to the suggestion of the tree I drew with words. We see in pictures and that is why even though I said "don't" people still saw the tree. In the workshop, if I then ask the participants to see oranges in the tree instead of apples, they can easily 'picture' it in their mind's eye. They have changed their perspective of the truth in an instant.

Because our mind sees in pictures, when conflict happens in the workplace, the more quickly it is resolved the less chance there will be for the parties involved to unconsciously take editorial license with the incident's facts. There will be less time for colleagues to ask questions and suggest, "Are you sure it was apples? It might have been oranges".

Memory expert and socio-linguist, Elizabeth Loftus suggests that *"Memories don't just fade...they grow. What fades is the initial perception, the actual experience of the events. But every time we recall an event, we must reconstruct the memory, and with each recollection the memory may be changed – colored by succeeding events, other people's recollections or suggestions... Truth and reality when seen through the filter of our memories, are not objective facts, but subjective, interpretative realities."*[3]

19

When police officers take information at a crime scene, they separate all the victims and witnesses and get their stories individually. This is because we focus in on different information. For example, was the coat black or brown? Was the perpetrator 6 ft or 5 ft 10 inches? When witnesses speak to each other, their perspectives are affected by the words of other witnesses. This is also why a police officer testifying in a court proceeding will often pull out notes to reference, as this information is the closest to the undiluted facts as possible.

The ability to distort is real and profound. When I am asked to be involved in writing a harassment prevention policy for an organization, I suggest that they include a short time frame to investigate and resolve the situation. Our mind is fluid, easily changed and rarely flawless.

To learn about our world, we create generalizations. We discussed earlier how we often learn beliefs from our parents and teachers. Another source of beliefs are generalizations. This is when we have one or few experiences with something and generalize this to be true for everything of that category. This is a key ingredient in our ability to learn, but this same unconscious skill can create inaccurate beliefs when applied to people instead of things.

Most of us have had the experience of driving a car with the gear shift on the steering column. When attempting to drive a vehicle with the gear shift on the floor, how did we know that the gear shift had the same purpose? Chances are that those handy letters D, R, P were also present. Car A is similar to Car B. A puts the car in gear. Perhaps B does as well.

Door knobs are usually round and located half way up the door. If we turn the knob and push, the door opens. If after years of round door knob experiences, what if we were to come across a rectangular door knob? How would we know what to do? A is similar to B. A opens the door. Maybe B does as well.

Generalizations can create beliefs about groups of people. Unfortunately, what works well with door knobs does not necessarily work well with people. If we have an experience of a person from a particular age, ability, ethnic or racial group, and we allow our mind to make that experience represent the entire group, we are in danger of generalizing. Although some may argue that this may give us some information 'in a general way' as to issues, needs or behaviours of a group, the danger of negating individuality for the sake of this argument is risky.

A friend in media tells me often that 'if it bleeds, it leads'. No news is no news and good news is no news. Death, murder, and scandal is what hits the news and many people who have no experience with people from certain groups may make judgments based on media alone. These judgments then become the beliefs from which we see that particular group.

It is ridiculous to think that every Muslim is a terrorist, yet if we have little or no experience with someone who is a Muslim, we are in danger of allowing the media to create our beliefs about this group. Following 9/11, the media fuelled a general fear of people who were Muslim or middle eastern. I have felt this as I have traveled through the United States since 9/11, listening to level orange alerts in airports where passengers are reminded to "notify officials if you see anyone suspicious". Who would look suspicious I wonder?[4] Would Timothy McVeigh, a white man, have looked suspicious?

Unlike the airplane crashes into the towers on 9/11, the July 2005 subway bombing in London in the U.K. has been followed by a different focus in the media. On Canadian media, Canadian Muslims have been interviewed and the difference between radical extremism and 'everyday' Canadian Muslims has become more apparent. On BBC (British television), leaders of Muslim communities and educational institutions have been informing viewers about how their community works and de-mystifying the activities of madressas[5] and mosques.

Unfortunately, until the crashes of 9/11, many Canadians' and Americans' only context around Muslims were those from the middle east. The ones that attend the mosque down the street were more a source of interest than a source of information. Even as Muslims across Canada have distanced themselves from the radical elements of Islam, for many people their beliefs about who a Muslim is have been cemented by the media following 9/11. Unless we question what Muslims believe and why, our beliefs will remain cemented.

If we get our information from media alone and do not monitor our ability to unconsciously generalize, it is a quick two-step to beliefs and negative stereotypes. **These beliefs and stereotypes about a group can lead to imbedded unconscious social and workplace consequences that disadvantage entire groups.**

Although men are usually willing to acknowledge that women have been disadvantaged in the workplace, particularly in the past, they are unlikely to acknowledge that they themselves have been over-privileged. Although Canadians of European descent are likely to acknowledge that visible minorities and aboriginal persons are disadvantaged in the workplace, they are less likely to acknowledge that they themselves have been over-privileged. This is because although we will work towards equity for groups we see as being treated inequitably, we don't wish to lessen our power or privilege in the same environment. As a white woman, sexism may put me at a disadvantage in the workplace, but white privilege puts me at an advantage.

Even suggesting that whites have been over-privileged leads many people to be uncomfortable, even angry. No one likes to think that their success is due to a 'leg-up' against their visible minority competition.

Although we are unconscious of this bag of unearned and hidden assets, we use them every day. They might include:

I can go shopping and not be followed around the store by a clerk.

I can turn on the TV or open the daily newspaper and see where people of my ethnicity have both positive and negative behaviours.

On TV documentaries of Canadian history, I can see that people of my colour and ethnicity existed and contributed.

Whether I use credit cards or cash, I can count on my skin colour not to work against the appearance of financial reliability.

I can criticize our government and talk about how much I fear or dislike a new policy without being seen as unappreciative of my country or a cultural outsider.

If I ask to talk to the manager or the person in charge, I will be facing a person of my race.

I can remain oblivious to the language and customs of persons of colour, who constitute the world's majority and a growing segment of Canadians, without feeling in my culture any penalty for such oblivion.

I am never asked to speak for all the people of my racial group.

I can do well in a challenging situation and not be a 'credit' to my race.

If a police or RCMP officer pulls me over, I can be sure I have not been singled out because of my race.

I can buy greeting cards, toys and magazines featuring people of my ethnicity.

I can belong to teams and committees in the workplace and feel connected as opposed to isolated or outnumbered.

I can take a job without having co-workers assume that I got the job because of my race and are not truly qualified.

I can travel and be assured that when I check into a hotel or rent a car, I will not be treated with disdain or distrust.

When I have an injury on the job, I can find bandages that match my skin tone.

Women have long discussed the 'old boys' network' and how it disadvantages women. As a woman I recognize the existence of the old boys' network, but as a white woman do I as quickly acknowledge the 'white women's network'? Do I recognize my advantage of being white as much as I recognize the colour disadvantage of a woman who is from a visible minority?

If white privilege exists, then there isn't really an even playing field. We must be constantly aware of our beliefs about others so that when we communicate, we are responding out of clear communication rather than reacting according to the agreements in place in our workplace, or the beliefs and stereotypes we personally hold.

ENDNOTES

1. Joseph Rudyard Kipling (1865-1936) was a British author and poet, born in India. He is best known for the children's story *The Jungle Book*, the Indian spy novel *Kim*, the poems *Gunga Din* and *If-*. He was also an outspoken defender of Western imperialism.

2. Five senses are visual (see), auditory (hear), kinesthetic (what we feel internally and externally), olfactory (smell) and gustatory (taste).

3. *Witness for the Defense: The Accused, the Eye Witness and the Expert Who Puts Memory On Trial* (1991) Elizabeth Loftus and K. Ketcham. Elizabeth Loftus is a world renowned memory expert and University of Washington psychology professor.

4. Timothy McVeigh was the Oklahoma City bomber. The Oklahoma City bombing was a 1995 terrorist attack in which the Alfred P. Murrah Federal Building, a U.S. government office complex in downtown Oklahoma City, Oklahoma, was destroyed, killing 168 people. It was the largest domestic terrorist attack in the history of the United States, and the second deadliest terrorist attack (after 9/11) in the nation's history.

At Timothy McVeigh's trial (a Gulf war veteran), the U.S Government asserted that the motivation for the attack was to avenge the deaths of Branch Davidians near Waco, Texas, that he believed had been murdered by agents of the federal government. McVeigh called the casualties in the bombing "collateral damage" and compared the bombing to actions he had taken during the Gulf War.

The effect of the bombing on the city was immense. Beyond the death toll of 168 (including 19 children and one rescue worker), the bomb injured over 800.

5. 'Madressas' are schools of Islamic religious learning.

CHAPTER FIVE
We Made It – Why Haven't They?

In the town of Tarnopol lived a man by the name of Reb Feivel. One day, as he sat in his house deeply absorbed in his Talmud[1], he heard a loud noise outside. When he went to the window he saw a lot of little pranksters. "Up to some new piece of mischief, no doubt", he thought.

"Children, run quickly to the synagogue", he cried, leaning out and improvising the first story that occurred to him. "You'll see that there is a sea monster, and what a monster! It's a creature with five feet, three eyes and a beard like that of a goat, only it's green!"

And sure enough the children scampered off and Reb Feivel returned to his studies. He smiled into his beard as he thought of the trick he had played on those little rascals. It wasn't long before his studies were interrupted again, this time by running footsteps. When he went to the window, he saw several Jews running.

"Where are you going?" he called out.

"To the synagogue", answered the Jews. "Haven't you heard? There is a sea monster with five legs, three eyes and a beard like a goat, only it's green!"

Reb Feivel laughed with glee, thinking of the trick he had played and sat down again to his Talmud. But no sooner had he begun to concentrate when suddenly he heard a dinning tumult outside. And what did he see? A great crowd of men, women and children, all running toward the synagogue.

"What's up?" he cried out of the window.

"What a question! Why don't you know?" they answered. "Right in front of the synagogue there's a sea monster. It's a creature with five legs, three eyes and a beard like that of a goat, only it's green." And as the crowd hurried by, Reb Feivel suddenly noticed that the rabbi himself was among them.

"Lord of the World!" he exclaimed. "If the rabbi himself is running with them surely there must be something happening. Where there's smoke there's fire." Without further thought Reb Feivel grabbed his hat, left his house, and also began running. 2

A Treasury of Jewish Folklore

When we believe anything about anything, we must ask "why"? Why do I believe what I do about Muslims, Jews, single mothers, gay men, aboriginal people, short people, obese people, detail focused people, people who stutter or people who prefer to work late rather than get up early?

We get our beliefs from generalizations and from people we hold in high esteem. In the previous chapter we discussed our generalizations. In the folk tale above, we can see how even when we know something may be incorrect, we will buy into an idea if someone we hold in esteem, such as a teacher or religious leader also believes it to be so.

The beliefs that we have about other groups impact our everyday communications with people who are different from us. We pre-judge who they are and their value to our organization or team, based on the stereotype we hold of the group they belong to, not the individual qualities and qualifications they possess.

We have inherited beliefs about aboriginal people and visible minorities. Across the country, descendants of Europeans have told their children about the hard won fight for survival in Canada. In fact, much of the cultural legend of Canada is highlighted by the struggle for survival and success in the less than friendly environment that the new immigrants adopted.

Many of the Canadians who inherited these stories cannot understand the on-going poverty and racism that exists in the country. They see that their families and ancestors have made it, why haven't others? Typically the question is really asked to imply that aboriginal people and some visible minorities lack the guts and determination or some other quality that is assumed to account for immigrant success in the past.

In the US, the Kerner Commission3 isolated five factors that explain why blacks had been unable to escape from poverty in the same way that European immigrants generations before had. Although this report was completed in 1968 and is American focused, many of its findings still ring true for Canada in the 21st Century.

Factor #1 – "The maturing economy – *Immigrants came at a time when the economy was undergoing a tremendous expansion and there was a drastic shortage of workers. Indeed, this is why North America opened its doors to so many immigrants in the first place. In contrast, American blacks have been coming to cities in a time when unskilled and semi-skilled jobs that provided an economic foothold for immigrants have been decreasing in number and importance making it much more difficult to get jobs and escape from poverty."*

Over 200,000 new immigrants come to Canada each year. Some are educated, speak English or French, and have professional credentials that are easily accepted. These new immigrants quickly move into a comfortable existence. Many other immigrants, however, who struggle with the language, have professional credentials that are not accepted without expensive upgrading or retraining, can easily fall into the abyss of unemployment or under-employment.

Factor #2 –"The disability of race – *Although European immigrants suffered from prejudice and discrimination, it was not as virulent or as pervasive as in the case of blacks. In the south, blacks were kept down by a ruthless system of exploitation and oppression. In the north, the industries that provided employment for millions of immigrants typically had a color line that excluded blacks altogether. Had blacks instead of immigrants been hired in the growing industries of the north, then we might today be* *asking why so few immigrants "made it" into the middle classes."*

For First Nations, *the Indian Act* and the permit and pass system made it difficult to access employment off the reserve, and employment on the reserve was minimal. Even after the permit and pass system was removed in the 1960s and Indians could move more freely in society, the lack of knowledge about the ways of the mainstream workplace was a disadvantage.

Factor #3 – "Entry into the political system – *Immigrants had political opportunity that never existed for blacks. Many immigrant groups have had their turn controlling urban political machines, but blacks have rarely controlled even their own communities, much less the enormous resources of urban government."*

Much of the political system in Canada has been controlled by those of European descent.

Consider that it wasn't until 1834 that slavery was formally abolished in Canada, so certainly those men and women did not have control or influence.

Women were legally excluded from voting until 1917 and then only if they met the requirements of an exception made for military personnel.4 By 1918, white women had the same right as white men to vote in federal elections.

Until 1947, Chinese Canadians were not allowed to vote federally and not in BC provincial elections until 1949.

Until 1960, Status Indians had to give up their treaty rights and registered Indian status in order to vote.

Factor #4 – "Cultural factors – *Immigrants were poor at a time when the standard of living was generally low, and they could look forward to a brighter future. As a consequence, they were able to maintain stable families and communities and a sense of optimism. Today, however, ghetto blacks are surrounded by affluence, and their prospects are bleak. It is hardly surprising that severe strains are placed on family and community and that the mood is often one of resignation and despair."*

Many early immigrants came to Canada with next to nothing. However, in Western Canada as well as other areas of the country, land was easily bought and often granted. Immigrant societies, such as Settlement House in the west, assisted new Canadians to adapt to the language and culture of the country. Many people arrived in groups to start new settlements and so had a 'we're all in this together' attitude.

Factor #5 – "A vital element of time – *Immigrants forget that when they were immersed in poverty, they too lived in slums that produced high rates of alcoholism, desertion, illegitimacy and other issues associated with poverty. It may take black Americans several generations to escape from poverty. The structure of opportunity is less favorable than in the past. What the American economy of the late 19th and early 20th centuries was able to do to help the European immigrant escape from poverty is now largely impossible."*

In an effort to investigate the inequities that exist in Canada, the Government of Canada struck a commission. In 1984, the Royal Commission on Equality found that four distinct groups were under-represented in the workplace. They were aboriginal people (Inuit, Indian and Métis), women$_5$, visible minorities and persons with disabilities.

In response to the Royal Commission on Equality, *the Employment Equity Act*$_6$ came into being in 1986. This made it possible for organizations to have special employment programs to attract and retain employees from the four equity groups. The goal was to have a representative work force, one that reflected the makeup of the working age population at different occupational levels.

According to a 2002 report of the Saskatchewan Human Rights Commission, special programs (employment equity plans) "are driven by both economic and philosophical goals. They promote harmony and prosperity in society as a whole, while pursuing fairness and equality for individuals."

Section 47 of *the Employment Equity Act* gives Human Rights Commissions the authority to approve programs designed to reduce disadvantages experienced by groups because of discrimination. It also gives the Human Rights Commissions the authority to monitor, vary, attach conditions to, or withdraw approval of any program approved under Section 47.

Section 47 states that nothing done in accordance with an approved program is a violation of the Human Rights Act itself and an employer with an approved employment equity plan seeking to increase the number of employees from the four equity groups can state a preference for such candidates in job advertisements. Programs approved by the human rights commissions are therefore modifications of the strict anti-discrimination provisions of the Human Rights Code.

Employment equity is a program that is more misunderstood than understood, even by our law makers, our federal politicians. The following letter to the editor was written by Jim Pankiw, Member of Parliament for Saskatoon-Humboldt:[6]

Takes Exception

"I take exception to the numerous recent articles in which I have been characterized as "disgusting", "boneheaded", "irresponsible", and according to Doug Cuthand, "a jerk".

It is unfortunate that I should be the recipient of such ad hominem attacks, simply because I have the virtue to expose a race-based native-preference hiring policy at the University of Saskatchewan.

It is interesting to note that journalists have resorted to exactly the type of politically correct rhetoric and doublespeak, to which I referred in my Jan. 6 letter to University of Saskatchewan President Peter MacKinnon, in order to justify this objectionable program.

For instance, they surreptitiously defend the goal of natives achieving a 12 per cent share of total jobs at the University while denying that there is a quota. However had the journalists bothered to pick up a dictionary, they would have discovered that a quota is, by definition, the share of a total.

Furthermore, had they bothered to research the issue, they would have dis-covered that job applicants to the University are classified as 'aboriginal' or 'non-aboriginal". The purpose of this classification becomes clear when we examine the University of Saskatchewan interim report on employment equity, which states: "the intent of the project is to be able to offer a recruiter a selected number of pre-screened candidates...who meet the university's employment equity goals." Translation: non-Indians will be screened out and therefore need not apply.

Proponents of this race-based hiring policy infer that discrimination is somehow acceptable because it is Indians perpetrating an injustice on non-Indians. However I find this notion disturbing in that it reflects the new math of socialist thinking: two wrongs somehow make a right.

I therefore urge all fair-minded Saskatchewan residents to join me in opposition to this insulting and offensive race-based program."

Jim Pankiw, MP

A day or so later, my response was published in the Letter to the Editor section of the same paper:

"I take exception to Mr. Pankiw's taking exception to the community holding him responsible for his comments. It is apparent from his Letter to the Editor on January 26th that he just doesn't get it – he doesn't understand Canadian legislation, demographics of Saskatchewan and the difference between American and Canadian equality initiatives.

It is almost amusing that we have a Member of Parliament that is not aware of the true nature of employment equity legislation (after all, it has only been around for 14 years). It is interesting that he used the term "exposed" regarding the hiring policy at the U of S. Wait til he finds out that most educational, government and large corporate organizations actually "publish" their employment equity plans – and publicly report how they plan to create an equal playing field within their organizations. How much easier his job will be!

The nature of the employment equity plans within organizations are to create an opportunity for the employees within that organization to reflect the diverse community they live in and the clients they serve. Therefore it makes sense that the U of S would have a long-term goal of 88% of their jobs being awarded to non-aboriginal people and 12% to aboriginal people. That is a reasonably fair assessment of population diversity within the province. Employment equity plans work towards goals of reflecting the outside world, whereby the US Affirmative action system is "quota" related with serious fines connected to the lack of achievement of those targets.

Also, employment equity plans often include employee training on how the country and organization is changing and how they can address their own biases and stereotypes. The point to embracing a diverse workforce is two-fold: representative employment is the 'right' thing to do' and most organizations now recognize that it makes good business sense.

Why we need goals and plans is because as human beings, we unconsciously hire people we trust, we trust people we like, and we like

31

people who are the most like us - and guess what? Most people with the power to hire at the U of S are NOT aboriginal. So we as a society have determined (thanks to the Royal Commission on Equality and the Employment Equity Act) that we need to make a conscious effort (often with specific goals) to include those who are different from the decision makers in an organization. As most senior positions are held by white males, this means - particularly in this province - that we need to be conscious of opportunities to hire aboriginal people into all kinds of positions.

Jeanne Martinson

Five years have passed since the MP's and my wild ride in the editorial pages, but the charge of reverse discrimination is still one that pops up, especially in my diversity seminars and respectful workplace workshops. A man in one workshop told me that he wanted to get into the RCMP but wasn't accepted. He was certain that if he was an aboriginal lesbian woman in a wheelchair he would have been accepted in a snap.

Reverse discrimination is addressed by Judge Abella in the Royal Commission on equality, "The end of exclusivity is not reverse discrimination, it is the beginning of equality. The economic advancement of women and minorities is not the granting of a privilege or advantage to them; it is the removal of a bias in favour of white males that has operated at the expense of other groups."

Although women and minorities (aboriginal and visible minorities) still remain underemployed and unemployed in higher numbers than the rest of the working population, employment equity appears to be a slow but steady remedy.

So if it is good for the country and good for organizations, why the strong negative response to employment equity?

One reason is perhaps the effect of the American model of affirmative action on our Canadian mindset. The American model and experience is very different from ours.

The United States model of affirmative action dates back to the Civil Rights Act of 1964 when court-imposed programs and strong enforcements were put into place. The process became statistical and enforcement agencies set quotas and timelines that were rigid and failure punishable. Formulas were based on equating the number of people in the general population with a proportionate number working for the organization, with little regard to ensuring ability. This created the potential of employees, who were not qualified, being hired and those in their work teams having no choice but to make do and pick up the slack.

The Canadian model of employment equity uses the word 'target'. We set numerical goals, but they are not quotas. This does not, therefore bind employers' hands and force them to hire people who they feel may not perform successfully on the job. Targets and goals are measures of progress toward the ultimate goal of equal employment opportunity.

Although we would like to think otherwise, there is also a personal reason for the strong response to employment equity. This reason has been around as long as more than one person has wanted a position:

> *Everytime I bestow a vacant office I make a hundred discontented persons and one ingrate.*

Louis XIV 1638-1715

> *For not many men, the proverb says, can love a friend whose fortune prospers without feeling envy; and about the envious brain, cold poison clings and doubles all the pain life brings him. His own woundings he must nurse and feel another's gladness like a curse.*

Aeschylus 525-456 BC

ENDNOTES

1. *The Talmud* is a combination of the Mishnah and the Gemara. This Jewish book of religion includes the entire *Torah* (first five books of the bible) or *Five Books of Moses* as well as other books of laws, guidelines and directions including the codified Oral Torah.

2. *A Treasury of Jewish Folklore*, Nathan Ausubel, Editor, 1948.

3. The Kerner Commission was created to report to president Lyndon Johnson on the recent 1967 race riots in the United States. Headed by Illinois governor Otto Kerner, its real leading spirit was John Lindsay, mayor of New York. Pessimistic in tone, its finding was that the riots resulted from black frustration at the lack of economic opportunity, and that America was becoming two societies, separate and unequal.

4. Women could vote before Confederation. Bluebirds (women in the service) stationed in Europe met those requirements, and were probably the very first women to vote legally in a Canadian federal election.

5. A minority group is not necessarily small. A minority group is sometimes made up of a majority of the members of a society – as in the case of blacks in South Africa and women in Canada.

'Minority' is used to refer to those people who have a disproportionately smaller share of the power and assets that are distributed in society. In the area of employment equity, women are referred to as being under-represented in areas of management and non-traditional roles.

6. *Regina Leader Post*, January 26, 2000.

CHAPTER SIX
We's, not Me's

In a previous book, *Escape from Oz – Leadership for the 21st Century*, I explored a model that included four key personal leadership areas: courage, insight, influence and self-discipline.

These cornerstones of leadership apply as well to the diversity ideas presented in this book.

In the Awareness section of this book, you have been challenged to re-think how you judge others whom you consider different from yourself.

The upcoming section, Understanding, will offer insight into the individual differences that can create conflict between people in the workplace.

The third section, Reconciliation, will discuss ways to influence others through reconciling behaviours.

The final section, Synergy, shows us that when we have the self-discipline to incorporate insight, influence and courage, we can experience a long-term positive impact in the workplace.

As you see in the diagram above, these four elements are held together by a band called 'trust'. It is easier for people in the workplace to trust you or the organization if they feel that you will step outside of previously held parameters in order to learn more about them and communicate with them based on who they are rather than who you think they should be.

As we become more knowledgeable about the different paths people have walked, we also need to be cognizant about what may be happening inside of ourselves. As we become more aware of diversity, there are four stages we transition through. Some of us go through them quickly, while others dwell for longer periods of time in a certain stage.

When we first have contact with people from a group with whom we don't identify, we may be oblivious to their issues. We see ourselves as part of the workplace and haven't particularly seen where the structure of the workplace inhibits the success of certain groups of people.

In the second stage, we expand our knowledge about matters that relate to other groups because we begin to have daily interactions with their members. This new-found knowledge challenges us to acknowledge our beliefs and examine our own cultural values. The most significant feature of this stage is our internal conflict between remaining within the comfortable norm and wishing to uphold personal values of fairness.

At the third stage, we identify with this diversity group. Even if we are not part of this minority group, we may still identify, assuming a special sensitivity to the cause of the person who is different, adopting a strong pro-minority stance. (Minority is defined in this case as a group with less power than other groups in a workplace, not necessarily a visible minority or a minority in a numerical sense.)

If we are not part of this minority, we may experience self-focused anger and guilt over previous conformity to the social and workplace norm. Our anger could also be directed outward to the society at large. This could lead to others challenging us on our pro-diversity views. They may even be angry at their perception of our disloyalty. Moreover, we may be confronted by people from the disadvantaged group who believe that we don't really know 'their reality'. As a result of this rejection from within and without, some of us may feel life would be easier and less complicated if we just hung out with people 'more like us'.

If we get stuck at any of these three stages, anger could spill over into intergroup hostility.

The last stage is when we redefine the 'new norm' and how we and others fit into it. In this stage, we confront our 'assumed sameness' of groups that are different from ourselves. We cease to define the best workplace as one made up of 'me's', but a workplace made up of 'we's".

CHAPTER SEVEN

From Nations to Tribes and Back Again

America, separated from Europe by a wide ocean, was inhabited by a distinct people, divided into separate nations, independent of each other and the rest of the world, having institutions of their own, and governing themselves by their own laws. It is difficult to comprehend...that the discovery of either by the other should give the discoverer rights in the country discovered which annulled the previous rights of its ancient possessors.

Chief Justice John Marshall, United States Supreme Court, Worcester v. Georgia (1832).[1]

Canada enjoys a reputation as a special place – a place where human rights and dignity are guaranteed, where democracy is respected, where diversity among people is celebrated.

But history shows that Canada was founded on a series of bargains with Aboriginal people – bargains Canada has never fully honoured. Treaties between Aboriginal and non-Aboriginal governments were agreements to share the land. They were replaced by policies intended to remove Aboriginal people from their homelands, suppress Aboriginal nations and their governments, undermine Aboriginal culture, and stifle Aboriginal identity.

These are strong words, but the evidence behind it is strong as well. By understanding the evidence of an Aboriginal person's past, we can better understand the Aboriginal people we work with every day.

Aboriginal people's living standards have improved in the past 50 years, but for many they do not come close to those of non-Aboriginal people. For aboriginal people in Canada, life expectancy is lower, illness is more common, family violence is more prevalent, and completing high school or attending college or university is more unlikely.

And now they are working with you. And they bring their history, as do you, into the workplace every day. Our differences can create conflict if we make assumptions about who each other is, what limits our success, what motivates us, and who we are in Canadian society.

To understand our present, we need to first look at the past. Many Canadians know little about the peaceful and co-operative relationship that grew between First Nations people and European visitors in the early years of contact. They know even less about how it changed, over the centuries, into something less honourable.

The relationship between Aboriginal and non-Aboriginal people has evolved through four stages: There was a time when Aboriginal and non-Aboriginal people lived on separate continents and knew nothing of one another. Following the years of first contact, initial relations of peace, friendship and equality were given the force of law in treaties. Then power tilted toward non-Aboriginal people and governments. The federal government moved Aboriginal people off much of their land and took steps to teach them European ways. We are now in the fourth stage – a time of recovery for Aboriginal people, a time for critical review of our relationship and a time for its renegotiation and renewal.

So how did we get to this point?

Prior to 1500 CE, Aboriginal societies in the Americas and non-Aboriginal societies in Europe developed along separate paths, in ignorance of one another. The variety in their languages, cultures and social traditions was enormous. Yet on both sides of the

Atlantic, independent nations with evolving systems of government flourished and grew. In the southeastern region of North America, the Cherokee were organized into a confederacy of some 30 cities – the greatest of which was nearly as large as London, UK at the time of first contact. Further south, in Central and South America, Indigenous peoples had carved grand empires out of the mountains and jungles long before Cortez arrived.

In Canada, Aboriginal cultures were shaped by the environment and the evolution of technology. The plentiful resources of the ocean and forest enabled west coast First Nations to build societies of wealth and sophistication. On the prairies and northern tundra, other nations lived in close harmony with vast, migrating herds of bison and caribou. In the forests of central Canada, aboriginal people harvested wild rice and grew corn, squash and beans, supplementing crops by fishing, hunting and gathering. On the east coast and in the far north, the bounty of the sea and land enabled First Nations people to survive in harsh conditions.

The Americas were not, as the Europeans told themselves when they arrived, terra nullius – empty land.

Encounters between Aboriginal and non-Aboriginal people began to increase in number and complexity in the 1500s. Early contact first involved mutual curiosity and apprehension, followed by a tentative exchange of goods. Barter and trade deals followed, and friendships and intermarriage created bonds between individuals and families. During this time military and trade alliances flourished, creating bonds between and among nations.

Non-Aboriginal accounts of early contact tend to emphasize the 'discovery and development' of North America by explorers. But this is a one-sided view. For at least 200 years, the newcomers would not have been able to survive the climate, or succeed in their businesses of fishing, whaling, or fur trading without the help of aboriginal people. Cautious co-operation, not conflict, was the theme of this period, which lasted into the 18th or 19th century. The different nations, European and First Nation, saw each other as separate, distinct and independent. Each was in charge of its own affairs and negotiated its own military alliances and trade deals. As different colonial powers attempted to dominate the North American continent, it became more and more important for colonists to align with Indian nations who could assist them in their struggle.

Treaties and Proclamations

This co-operation was formalized in two important ways. One was *the Royal Proclamation of 1763*. The other was in treaties set down in writing by British, French and other European negotiators and affirmed by Aboriginal nations in oral and visual records, such as wampum belts.

A bed of white wampum symbolizes the purity of the agreement. There are two rows of purple, and those two rows represent the spirit of our ancestors. Three beads of wampum separating the two purple rows symbolize peace, friendship and respect. The two rows of purple are two vessels traveling down the same river together. One, a birch bark canoe, is for the Indian people, their laws, their customs and their ways. The other, a ship, is for the white people and their laws, their customs and their ways. We shall each travel the river together, side by side, but in our own boat. Neither of us will try to steer the other's vessel. 2

The description of the Two Row Wampum belt that commemorated the 1613 treaty between the Mohawk and the Dutch captures the understanding of Aboriginal peoples of treaties. Treaties were statements of peace, friendship, sharing or alliance, not submission or surrender.

The Royal Proclamation of 1763 was an important document in the relationship between Aboriginal and non-Aboriginal people in North America. Issued in the name of the king, the proclamation summarized the rules that were to govern British dealings with Aboriginal people – especially in relation to the key question of land. It is a complex legal document, but the central messages are clear. Aboriginal people were not to be "molested or disturbed" on their lands. Transactions involving Aboriginal land were to be negotiated properly between the Crown and "assemblies of Indians". Aboriginal lands were to be acquired only by treaty or purchased by the Crown.

The proclamation portrays Indian nations as autonomous political entities, living under the protection of the Crown but retaining their own internal political authority. It walks a fine line between safeguarding the rights of Aboriginal peoples and establishing a process to permit British settlement. It finds a balance in an arrangement allowing Aboriginal and non-Aboriginal people to divide and share sovereign rights to the lands that are now Canada.

From independent nations to controlled bands

So how did we get from this respectful co-existence, where Canada was a country made up of nations, to one where Indians were dominated by non-Aboriginal laws and institutions and nations destroyed?

In the 1800s, the relationship between Aboriginal and non-Aboriginal people began to tilt on its foundation of equality. The number of settlers was swelling, and so was their power. As immigrants dominated the land, so they came to dominate its original inhabitants. They no longer needed the Indians to survive in the new country.

Settlers gained power as a result of four changes that were transforming the country: 3

1. The population mix was shifting to favour the settlers. Immigration continued to add to their numbers, while poverty and illness caused by European diseases that Indians could not tolerant decimated their numbers. By 1812, immigrants outnumbered Aboriginal people in Upper Canada by a factor of ten to one.

2. The fur trade was dying, and with it the old economic partnership between traders and trappers. The new economy was based on timber, minerals, agriculture. It needed land – not labour from Aboriginal people, who began to be seen as impediments to progress instead of valued partners.

3. Colonial governments in Upper and Lower Canada no longer needed Aboriginal nations as military allies. The British had defeated the French and the continent was at peace.

4. An ideology proclaiming European superiority over all other peoples of the earth was taking hold. It provided a rationale for

policies of domination and assimilation, which slowly replaced partnership in the North American colonies.

The treaties and *Royal Proclamation of 1763* that theoretically offered Aboriginal people peace, friendship, respect, and equality, also provided 'protection'. At first, it meant preservation of Aboriginal lands and cultural integrity from encroachment by settlers. It later became the excuse for negative strategies such as compulsory residential schools, physical and economic control with the permit/pass system by federal agents, and restrictions on practicing traditions and religion.

Colonial and Canadian governments established reserves of land for Aboriginal people with or without treaty agreements. The system began in 1637, with a Jesuit settlement at Sillery in New France. Reserves were designed to protect Aboriginal people and preserve their ways, but often had the effect of creating isolation and poverty.

Confederation, in 1867, was a new partnership between English and French colonists to manage lands and resources north of the 49th parallel. It was negotiated without reference to Aboriginal nations, the first partners of both the French and the English. *The British North America Act*, Canada's new constitution, made "Indians, and lands reserved for the Indians" a subject for government regulation, like mines or roads. Parliament passed laws to replace traditional Aboriginal governments with band councils with minimum powers, took control of resources located on reserves and reserve finances, imposed an unfamiliar system of land tenure, and applied non-Aboriginal concepts of marriage and parenting.

These laws, and others, were codified in *the Indian Acts* of 1876, 1880, 1884 and later.

The Department of the Interior (today known as Department of Indian and Northern Development or DIAND) sent Indian agents to every region to see that the laws were obeyed. The impact of these laws and their enforcement changed the lives of Indians forever.

Cultural genocide

In 1884, the potlatch ceremony, central to the cultures of west coast Aboriginal nations, was outlawed. Until 1957, an amendment to *the Indian Act* instituted prison sentences for anyone participating in potlatch, tawanawa dance and other traditional aboriginal ceremonies.

In 1885, the sun dance, central to the cultures of prairie Aboriginal nations, was outlawed. Participation was a criminal offense.

Physical control

In 1885, the Department of Indian Affairs instituted a pass system. Section 32(1) of *the Indian Act* states: "A transaction of any kind whereby a band or member purports to sell, barter, exchange, give or otherwise dispose of cattle... grain, hay... to a person other than a member of the band is void unless the superintendent approves the transaction in writing."

This meant that no outsider could come onto a reserve to do business with an Aboriginal resident without permission from the Indian agent. In many places, *the Indian Act* was interpreted to mean that no Aboriginal person could leave the reserve without permission from the Indian agent. Reserves were beginning to resemble prisons.

Ward of the state

Indians in most parts of Canada had the right to vote, but only if they gave up their treaty rights and Indian status through a process defined in *the Indian Act* as 'enfranchisement'. The exception to this was that the vote was extended in 1924 to Aboriginal veterans of WWI, including veterans living on Indian reserves.

Aboriginal people were unenthusiastic about having the right to vote if it meant giving up their individual and group identity. Thus, until the government of Canada under John Diefenbaker extended the vote to Indian persons unconditionally in 1960, there is little evidence that First Nations people sought the vote.

Métis and Inuit people were not excluded from voting.

Residential schools

In 1879 Conservative MP, Nicholas Flood Davin was sent to the US to study the Indian education system and its appropriateness as a model for western Canada. Davin recommended the establishment of federally-funded, church-run boarding schools to teach Indian children Christian morality and work habits away from the influence of their home.4

Between the 1880s and 1990s, 25%-30% of Indians attended government residential schools. Others attended day schools, and some did not go to school at all. Many of the residential schools prohibited the students from practicing their culture, speaking their language, and keeping in touch with their family. In 1920, attendance at residential school became mandatory by law for Indian children (this was later repealed). As more parents became aware of the abuse at the schools, this often meant the RCMP taking children from their parents by force.

May 19, 2004:

Giuliano Zaccardelli, Canada's Commissioner for the RCMP made an emotional apology to First Nations communities for the 'personal pain and distress' of abuse during the terrible chapter in Canadian history when natives were forced into residential schools and stripped of their culture. "That is the history that cannot be forgotten but must be overcome, he said."5

By 1958, there were 37,000 children enrolled in residential schools. In 1969, the federal government took over administration of the schools from the churches and decided to start winding down the system. Ten years later, only 15 schools remained across Canada.

In 1991, the Missionary Oblates of Mary Immaculate became the first religious order to apologize for their role in the residential schools. The Anglicans apologized in 1993, followed by the Presbyterians in 1994. The Gordon School in Saskatchewan was the last federally run Indian residential school in Canada when it closed its doors in 1996.

"Residential schools did the greatest damage. Children as young as 6 years old were removed from their families for 10 months

of the year or longer. They were forbidden to speak the only languages they knew and taught to reject their homes, their heritage and, by extension, themselves. Most were subjected to physical deprivation, and some experienced abuse. We heard from a few people who are grateful for what they learned at these schools, but we heard from more who described deep scars – not least in their inability to give and receive love."6

Land movement and seizure

During the third stage in the changing relationship, the Canadian government moved Aboriginal communities from one place to another at will. If Aboriginal people were thought to have too little food, they could be relocated where game was more plentiful or jobs might be found. If they were suffering from illness, they could be relocated to new communities where health services, sanitary facilities and permanent housing might be provided. If they were in the way of expanding agricultural frontiers, or in possession of land needed for settlement, they could be relocated 'for their own protection'. If their lands contained minerals to be mined, forests to be cut, or rivers to be dammed, they could be relocated 'in the national interest'.

Chief Poundmaker's great-nephew, John Tootoosis was 25 years old when the local Indian agent tried to lease five sections of Poundmaker reserve to a white farmer. He went to see a lawyer who told him that if the land were fenced the lease could be blocked. Tootosis went back to the reserve, organized a work party and put up the fence. When he became active in talking to other bands about how to ensure that their land did not get siphoned off, he was threatened with trespass by Indian Affairs.7

Even when First Nations were able to keep hold of reserved land, the government sometimes sold its resources to outsiders. These disappearances took place despite the solemn duty of the Crown to manage lands and resources for the benefit of First Nations people. Reserve land was steadily whittled away after its original allocation. Almost two-thirds of it has 'disappeared' by various means since Confederation. In some cases, the government failed to deliver as much land as specified in a treaty. In other cases, it expropriated or sold reserved land, rarely with First Nations as willing vendors. Once in a while, outright fraud took place.

The need for welfare in Aboriginal communities came with the confiscation of ever expanding tracts of their land. Indigenous people grew poor, malnourished and sick. Many died young. The government chose to provide short-term relief instead of sustained help to rebuild ravaged First Nations economies – a choice governments have made over and over again in the last two centuries.

Veteran neglect and vote denial

Up to 8000 aboriginal people joined the Canadian military in WWI, WWII, Korea, Vietnam or for peacekeeping duties. Non-Indian returning WWII veterans received a parcel of land with clear title, $6,000, spousal benefits, education and jobs. For returning Indians, it was a much different story. All they received was money to a maximum of $2,320. Had native veterans received the same compensation as non-native veterans, its value would have been $125,000 – $400,000 according to estimates by financial experts. [8]

It took until 2003 for the government of Canada to offer a settlement of $20,000 per veteran (and only if they signed away their rights to sue for further compensation). [9]

No Canadian acquainted with the policies of domination and assimilation would wonder why Aboriginal people distrust the good intentions of non-Aboriginal people and their governments today.

The way back to nationhood

Policies of domination and assimilation battered Aboriginal institutions, sometimes to the point of collapse. Poverty, ill health and social disorganization grew worse. Aboriginal people struggled for survival as individuals, their nationhood erased from the public mind and almost forgotten by themselves.

Resistance to assimilation grew weak, but it never died away. In the fourth stage of the relationship, it caught fire and began to grow into a political movement. One stimulus was the federal government's White Paper on Indian policy (issued in 1969) that proposed to abolish *the Indian Act* and all that remained of the special relationship between Aboriginal people and Canada. First Nations were nearly unanimous in their rejection. They saw the White Paper as an attempt to end their existence as distinct peoples. Together with Inuit and Métis, they began to realize the full significance of their survival in the face of sustained efforts to assimilate them.

A dozen years of intense political struggle by Aboriginal people, including appeals to the Queen and the British Parliament, produced an historic breakthrough. "Existing Aboriginal and Treaty Rights" were recognized in *the Constitution Act, 1982*. This set the stage for profound change in the relationship among the peoples of Canada.

The policies of the past failed to bring peace and harmony to the relationship between Aboriginal peoples and other Canadians. Equally, they failed to bring contentment or prosperity to Aboriginal people.

Successive governments have tried – sometimes intentionally, sometimes in ignorance – to eliminate Aboriginal people as distinct peoples. Policies have undermined and erased much of Aboriginal culture and identity.

Assimilation policies have done great damage, leaving a legacy of brokenness affecting Aboriginal individuals, families and communities. The damage has been equally serious to the spirit of Canada – the spirit of generosity and mutual accommodation in which Canadians take pride.

Ongoing Issues of Misunderstanding

Who is an Indian anyway?

The Aboriginal peoples of Canada include three groups:

First Nations people (commonly and legally referred to as Indian). They are registered on a list at the Department of Indian Affairs and Northern Development (DIAND) and therefore have "status" whether they live on a reserve or off. They are members of the various First Nations or "bands" across Canada, of which there are about 640, with approximately 2,500 reserves across Canada. The current on-reserve population is about 400,000 and

49

off-reserve population is about 200,000. Projections by DIAND for total population by 2020 is over 905,000.

Prior to the changes made by Bill C31 in 1985, Indians lost their rights and status as an Indian if they earned a university degree or (if female) married a non-status Indian. In 1985, this *Act to Amend the Indian Act* brought these two exceptions back into status and into alignment with *the Canadian Charter of Rights and Freedoms.*

The Inuit people number approximately 45,000 and live primarily in their new territory of Nunavut and in the Northwest Territories.

The Métis have close to one million in population and are spread coast to coast with the greatest population in the Prairies. This group frequently includes those Indians who have lost 'status' for some reason and are unable to recover it.

A Métis person is defined as a person who is:

– of mixed Aboriginal and non-Aboriginal ancestry but does not have Indian status under *the Indian Act,*

– is registered as Métis by the Métis community,

– has ancestors who were entitled to receive land grants or script under the provisions of *the Manitoba Act* of 1870 or *the Dominion Lands Act,*

– can prove they are Métis.

They don't pay taxes, do they?

All Métis and non-status Indians pay federal and provincial sales tax as well as federal and provincial income taxes.

Status or treaty Indians (not all Indians are covered by treaty) pay federal and provincial income taxes for any income they earn at jobs off the reserve. As most jobs are off-reserve, most income made by First Nations people is therefore taxable. Status Indians do not pay federal or provincial sales taxes on personal and real property bought on a reserve. GST must be paid on items bought off-reserve and depending on the province, Indians may or may not have to pay provincial sales tax on goods bought off-reserve.[10]

What about land claims?

There are two kinds of land claims:

1. Comprehensive land claims, based on the concept of continuing Aboriginal rights and title which have not been dealt with by treaty or other legal means. Comprehensive land claims are made when First Nations go to court to have governments recognize their rights to land and resources that were not given up in a treaty or other agreement. A series of court decisions (such as the landmark Nisga'a deal in B.C.) has confirmed that Aboriginal peoples have a legal right as well as a moral case for redress on land and resource issues.[11]

2. Specific land claims arising from non-fulfillment of Indian treaties and other lawful obligations or from the improper administration of lands and other assets under *the Indian Act*. Specific land claims are when a band has had their reserve land reduced illegally.

What if we had done what we promised?

If what First Nations people thought they had agreed upon had been delivered – a reasonable share of lands and resources for their exclusive use, protection for their traditional economic activities, resource revenues from shared lands, and support for their participation in the new economy being shaped by the settlers – the position of Aboriginal peoples in Canada today would be very different. They would be major land owners. Most Aboriginal nations would likely be economically self-reliant. Some would be prosperous.

In spite of history, everywhere in Canada there is evidence that aboriginal people are succeeding:

• The Membertou First Nation in Sydney, Nova Scotia joint ventured with companies like Clearwater FPI for seafood processing, jobs and their own brand, Membertou Crab.

• The national magazine, Windspeaker, produces inspiring stories of aboriginal business success and current news.

• Bigstone Cree Nation in Alberta created Bigstone Forestry Inc. by Slave Lake.

- Dakota Dunes Golf and Country Club near Saskatoon, Saskatchewan run by the Whitecap Dakota Sioux Nation

- Western Lakota Energy Services with partnerships from Dene Tha' First Nation, Samson Cree Nation Blood Tribe, Saddle Lake First Nation, Métis Nation of Alberta, Duncan First Nation and Horse Lake First Nation.

Employment in other businesses for aboriginal people are becoming the norm. Organizations like Serco Facilities Management (Ottawa), Exel Global Logistics (Montreal), Nassittuq (Ottawa), Cameco (Saskatoon), and Cogema (Saskatoon) all have more than a 10% aboriginal workforce. [12]

The ability to construct an identity for the self, either as an individual or as a collective, lies at the heart of modernity. I now see a group of [Aboriginal] people who are constructing a positive identity for themselves, who now see themselves as an integral part of, and contributors to, the society around them.

David Newhouse, Trent University [13]

A final note

There is beginning to be evidence for acknowledging the injustices of the past. But just as the restoration of Aboriginal nations and cultures appear to be offering real hope for renewed well-being, a backlash is developing – a reaction characterized by slogans like 'all Canadians are equal' and 'no special status'.

However, Aboriginal people have historical rights as self-governing political entities – rights that Canada undertook to safeguard as we were struggling toward nationhood. Ignoring this is the modern equivalent of the mind-set that led to *the Indian Act*, the residential schools, the forced relocations – and the other 19th century instruments of assimilation.

ENDNOTES

1. *Report of the Royal Commission on Aboriginal Peoples: People to people, nation to nation.*

2. *Report of the Royal Commission on Aboriginal Peoples: People to people, nation to nation.*

3. *Report of the Royal Commission on Aboriginal Peoples: People to people, nation to nation.*

4. "Canada's Dirty Little Secret" *Regina Leader Post*, Monday August 9, 2004.

5. "RCMP,AFN Sign Co-operation Plan" *Regina Leader Post*, May 19th, 2004.

6. *Report of the Royal Commission on Aboriginal Peoples: People to people, nation to nation.*

7. "Nine Who Made A Difference" *The Beaver/Canada's History Magazine*, August/September 2005.

8. "Native War Veterans Offered $20K" *National Post*, June 22, 2002.

9. "Indian Vet Continues Fight" *Regina Leader Post*, February 12, 2003.

10. Indian and Northern Affairs Canada website.

11. "The Final Agreement", *Globe and Mail*, Friday, December 10, 1999.

12. *Report of the Royal Commission on Aboriginal Peoples: People to people, nation to nation.*

13. "Aboriginal Voices" *Canadian Business*, March 29-April 11, 2004.

Name	Total population	Aboriginal pop.[1]	N. American Indian	Métis	Inuit	Non-Aboriginal population
Canada	29,639,030	976,305	608,850	292,305	45,070	28,662,725
NL	508,080	18,775	7,040	5,480	4,560	489,300
PE	133,385	1,345	1,035	220	20	132,040
NS	897,565	17,010	12,920	3,135	350	880,560
NB	719,710	16,990	11,495	4,290	155	702,725
QC	7,125,580	79,400	51,125	15,855	9,530	7,046,180
ON	11,285,545	188,315	131,560	48,340	1,375	11,097,235
MB	1,103,700	150,045	90,340	56,800	340	953,655
SK	963,155	130,185	83,745	43,695	235	832,960
AB	2,941,150	156,225	84,995	66,060	1,090	2,784,925
BC	3,868,875	170,025	118,295	44,265	800	3,698,850
YT	28,520	6,540	5,600	535	140	21,975
NT	37,100	18,730	10,615	3,580	3,910	18,370
NU	26,665	22,720	95	55	22,560	3,945

[1]Includes the Aboriginal groups (North American Indian, Métis and Inuit), multiple Aboriginal responses and Aboriginal responses not included elsewhere.
The Aboriginal identity population comprises those persons who reported identifying with at least one Aboriginal group, that is, North American Indian, Métis or Inuit, and/or who reported being a Treaty Indian or a Registered Indian, as defined by the Indian Act of Canada, and/or who reported being a member of an Indian Band or First Nation.

Population reporting an Aboriginal identity, by age group, by provinces and territories (2001 Census)

	Canada	QC	ON	MB	SK
Total	**976,305**	**79,400**	**188,315**	**150,040**	**130,185**
0-4 years	102,610	7,580	17,160	18,000	16,785
5-9 years	113,075	8,090	20,165	18,985	17,885
10-14 years	108,270	7,840	18,320	17,085	16,855
15-19 years	92,985	6,700	16,575	14,400	13,395
20-24 years	76,080	6,085	14,150	11,615	10,570
25-34 years	148,550	11,780	28,745	22,890	18,870
35-44 years	145,855	12,130	31,710	20,820	16,355
45-54 years	96,365	9,240	20,925	13,305	9,890
55-64 years	52,830	5,405	11,935	7,410	5,375
65 years and over	39,680	4,555	8,630	5,540	4,210

Source: Statistics Canada, Census of Population. Last modified: 2005-01-26.

CHAPTER EIGHT
Welcome to Barneyland!

"During the past decade, three key factors have shaped the nation's workforce: an increasing demand for skills in the face of advancing technologies and the knowledge-based economy, a working-age population that is increasingly made up of older people, and a growing reliance on immigration as a source of skills and labour force growth.

From 1991 to 2001, the number of people in the labour force increased by 1.3 million (+9.5%) to 15.6 million. Canada has increasingly turned to immigration as a source of skills and knowledge. Census data show that immigrants who landed in Canada during the 1990s, and who were in the labour force in 2001, represented almost 70% of the total growth of the labour force over the decade. If current immigration rates continue, it is possible that immigration could account for virtually all labour force growth by 2011."[1]

The continuous flow of foreigners coming to our shores has been integral to Canada's success. In the beginning, it wasn't about immigration to develop a new land. It was about resources, sovereignty claims for their home nation, and just dumb luck.

"Welcome to Barneyland!" That might be what we would say instead of "Welcome to Canada!" if Barney had only come ashore.

A Viking saga tells of an island trader named Bjarni (Barney) Herjolfsson, around CE 985 who returned home from Europe to find his father had left for a new settlement on Greenland. Barney set off west to follow and was blown off course in the fog. He landed in a new country with lots of trees and small hills. Barney did not go ashore. He realized his navigational error and turned around.2 He did however tell the tale of his misadventure. Perhaps it started, "You think *you've* made a wrong turn!!"

Leif Ericson (the son of Eric the Red who founded the Greenland colony) bought Barney's boat and sailed in a southwesterly direction from Greenland. When he landed he called the place Vinland (which means land of grapes, or berries, or meadows – depending who you ask). This first documented contact3 in 1000 CE was between the Norse and either the Dorset or Beothuk natives in Labrador. The Vikings' brief and gloomy stay is recorded in Norse myth. They built sod houses on the coast and repaired their ships using local iron deposits. Other Vikings made the trip to the tiny settlement as well. The natives brought furs to trade for metal implements, but the Vikings were hesitant to give them weapons. The relationship soured and the Vikings were forced to abandon the settlement.4

What if Portugal had taken more decisive action over their awarded territories? We might be speaking Portuguese as our official language today.

In 1493 Pope Alexander VI established a line of demarcation between Spanish and Portuguese territory5 in present day Canada. The lands to the west of this uncertain line were to be a Spanish monopoly and lands east, including Newfoundland and present day Nova Scotia, were to be Portuguese territory.

In 1501 and 1502, the Portuguese brothers Gaspar and Miguel Corte Real mapped an extensive portion of the North American seaboard. European cartographers felt free to name what lands they encountered and evidence of the Portuguese endeavors dot maps of Canada today with names such as the Bay of Fundy (Portuguese for deep bay) and Labrador (Lavrador meaning farmer).

But the Papal Bull6 of 1493 was to divide the land between Spain and Portugal and the English and French felt they had no duty to uphold an agreement they were not part of. As they say, possession is 9/10ths of the law, so when Cabot arrived in 1497 in clearly Portuguese territory he only had to follow his own Charter from England's Henry VII. His charter specified that he could not enter lands already discovered by the Portuguese so to the British this meant, unless there was obvious previous occupation, they were welcome to the territory.

Around 1521, a few dozen Portuguese families landed on the shores of the new world. They were armed with a charter from King Manuel of Portugal to establish a colony that could serve as a base for industry and trade. The settlers represented a last desperate attempt by the Portuguese to assert their claim to North America. Their colony predates the settlement of Port-Royal, which is considered to be Canada's first permanent European settlement, by more than 80 years. Unfortunately, the colony disappeared and no one knows for sure what became of Portugal's last ditch attempt.7

The prolific fishing off Newfoundland kept several European countries hovering about the shores of Canada. However, the desire for further resources eventually drove the French and English into more permanent relationships with the land and the people who already lived there.

As Europeans began settling in Canada, so too began our love/hate relationship with immigration. Who should come in? From where? Where should they settle? What kinds of jobs do we need them to do? How will it affect those who already live here? Who should get rights? Who should control the economic, religious and political power of the new land?

There have been three distinctive waves of immigration to Canada in the past 500 years.

The initial wave was of farmer settlers, missionaries and fur traders, primarily from France, England and Scotland.

The second wave, beginning around 1870, consisted mainly of immigrants from Europe to settle western Canada and build eastern Canadian infrastructure and industry. In this same time period, immigrants were also sought from China, primarily to build the railroad.

In our third and current wave of immigration, immigrants are sought based on a point system, not on country of origin. New immigrants are more likely to be from non-European countries and be visible minorities. In the enclosed data following the endnotes, notice the origins of Canada's 5,448,480 immigrant population as of 2001:

2,2287,555 are from Europe (UK, Northern, Western Europe, Eastern and Southern Europe)

1,989,180 are from Asia (West Central Asia and Middle East, Eastern Asia, Southeast Asia and Southern Asia)

282,600 and 294,050 from Africa and Caribbean or Bermuda respectively

304,650 from South and Central America

237,920 from the United States

So clearly, immigration is not new to Canada. Neither are immigration issues, racism or negative government policy. Canadians have short memories. We easily forget the influences of the immigrants before us, often seeing our own group as being highly positive, influential, yet at the same time discriminated against and minimized.

Consider these groups and events that have come and gone from memory:

The Acadian village of Grand Pré 250 years ago was the scene of the deportation of 10,000 men, women and children. Their colony had changed hands from British to French and back again many times since their arrival in 1604 and so the Acadians were cautious in their commitment to either side. They professed neutrality in the ongoing conflicts and were deported by the British to the American colonies. Virginia refused them so they were packed on ships and sent to British detention centres. In Georgia and South Carolina, they became indentured farm labourers. Maryland shot Acadians on sight and New York indentured them to Anglo-American settlers. 7500 to 9000 died either during deportation or trying to escape it. Many eventually settled in Louisiana where French Catholic settlers were welcome. It wasn't until 1766 that a group was allowed to settle in Quebec with equal treatment under the law. In New Brunswick, it wasn't until 1830 that the French were legal with equal political rights and in 1963, the first French language university opened in Moncton. The students attending there today have forgotten much of the past and take for granted survival and equal rights for Francophones. 8

When we think about Black Canadians we usually think about new immigrants, but Blacks in Canada have a longer history than that. Slavery existed in this country for over 100 years until it was finally abolished in 1834. Canadians did not refer to the term "slave", but used the term "servant." Slavery was established in Quebec, by the French, through a royal mandate issued by Louis XIV in 1689. This mandate not only gave permission to "Canadians to avail themselves of the services of African slaves", but declared as well that "all negroes who had been so bought or held should belong to the person so owning them, in full proprietorship". It was not unusual to see ads appear in the newspaper for slaves. *"The Nova Scotia Gazette and Weekly Chronicle"*, March 28, 1775, carried the following for sale item: "a likely, well-made negro boy, about sixteen years old." The same paper, in January 1779, advertised the sale of "an able Negro wench, about 21 years of age, capable of performing both town and country work." Between 1783-1784, 1232 Black slaves were brought by British masters into Nova Scotia, New Brunswick and Prince Edward Island. Slavery in Canada did not flourish economically as in America and began to decline at the beginning of the 19th century. When slaves were legally emancipated as of August 1, 1834, there were very few slaves in British North America who had not already obtained their legal freedom. 9

In 1872, the government of British Columbia denied the Chinese the right to vote and made it illegal for Chinese people to be employed on construction projects paid for by the provincial government. From 1880-1885, the construction of the western section of the Canadian Pacific Railway employed thousands of Chinese workers, but following its completion the federal government introduced *the Act to Restrict and Regulate Chinese Immigration into Canada*, which required that Chinese people entering Canada pay a head tax of $50 per person. The head tax was raised to $100 in 1902 and to $500 in 1903. In 1918, Ontario, Manitoba, Saskatchewan and British Columbia passed laws making it illegal to hire white women in Chinese-owned businesses. By 1919, Vancouver had 6000 Chinese with 210 families, and Toronto had 2100 Chinese with 35 families. In 1923, *the Chinese Immigration Act* (the Exclusion Act) prohibited Chinese immigrants from entering Canada. All Chinese people already living in Canada, even those born here, had to register with the government to receive a certificate of registration. Wives and children in China were unable to join their husbands and fathers in Canada. Chinese men were left with the difficult choice of staying in Canada alone and sending their meager earnings back to their poorer families or leave Canada and return to a life of poverty for their whole family. Finally in 1947, the Exclusion Act was repealed, Chinese Canadians were given the right to vote in federal elections and allowed to own businesses or work as pharmacists, lawyers and accountants.

After the entry of Great Britain into WWI, the government of Canada issued an order in council which provided for the registration and in certain cases for the internment of aliens of "enemy nationality". Many Ukrainian Canadians found themselves described as "enemy aliens". Most of the 171,000 Ukrainians living in Canada were settled in the Prairie region with some communities in Ontario and Quebec, where Ukrainians worked in the timber, mining, and construction industries. Since these immigrants had generally come to Canada from the Austrian crownlands of Galicia and Bukovyna, their citizenship, but not their nationality, could be described as "Austrian" or "Austro-Hungarian". Those so categorized were, under the terms of the same *War Measures Act of 1914*, subject to imprisonment in one of 26 receiving stations and internment camps established across Canada or at least to registration as "enemy aliens". Between 1914 and 1920, over 5000 Canadians of Ukrainian descent were incarcerated, among them women and children. Over 80,000 Ukrainians were categorized as "enemy aliens" and obliged to report regularly to their local police authorities or to the North West Mounted Police. They were issued with identity papers that had to be carried at all times, the penalty for noncompliance being arrest and imprisonment.

On February 26, 1942 (after Japan bombed Pearl Harbor) the Canadian government removed all Japanese Canadians living within 160 km of the BC coast, claiming a threat to national security. In all 20,881 people were sent to detention camps in the BC interior, and to sugar beet farms in Alberta and Manitoba. After the war, the internees were encouraged to return to Japan, even though most of them had been born in Canada.[10]

Despite this less than honourable past and ongoing issues, our country is still seen as a great cultural and racial equalizer, where anyone has a chance to be successful, safe and free.

As evidence of this, in 2004, Archbishop Desmond Tutu, the 14th Dalai Lama, and 2003 Nobel Peace Prize Winner Shirin Ebadi spoke at the Vancouver Christ Church Cathedral. The three great voices of global responsibility came together to discuss how to bring peace and freedom to the planetary neighbourhood and they "chose to do so not in London or Paris or New York but in Canada. Canada has become the spiritual home of the very notion of an extended emancipating, global citizenship."[11]

"The retirement of the baby boomers is in the near future and there will be a greater demand for the social programs we value, particularly healthcare. At the same time there will be fewer people working and therefore contributing to those same programs. We will begin to see the ratio drop from about five workers for each retired person to about 2.5 to one."

Ralph Goodale, Canada's Minister of Finance speaking about the need for more skilled immigrants to Canada[12]

We are a welcoming country to new immigrants and we obviously need them. So who is coming to Canada today and what are our ongoing issues minimizing their success?

For its size, Canada is in a class by itself. In 2001, it absorbed more than 250,000 permanent residents. The US and Australia take in only half as many immigrants per capita. In 2001, Canada welcomed 153,000 economic immigrants (including accompanying family members), 27,800 refugees and 66,600 people who were accepted because they were the children, parents, grandparents, spouses or fiancés of existing residents.

The high numbers are a mixed blessing. In 2001, 77% of newcomers poured into Vancouver, Montreal and Toronto, more than 125,000 settling in Toronto alone. Fully 44% did not speak English or French. But almost 60% of adult immigrants in 2000 had a post secondary degree compared to 43% of the existing population of Canada.

Ongoing Issues

Desire for cultural acknowledgement

Following WWII, Toronto's Anglo-Saxon and Northern European ethnic mix was transformed with the arrival of successive waves of Southern European immigrants. Until the 1970s, however, few residents of Toronto had much direct experience with "race" – routine daily encounters with persons distinguished by their skin colour. Since the 1970s, the source countries for immigrants to Canada shifted from Europe to Asia, Africa, the Middle East, the Caribbean, and Central and South America. Between 1981 and 1996 the estimated visible minority population of Toronto rose from 14% to 32% and the percentage of children of visible minority families increased from 16% to 38%.

Historically new immigrants that are young with limited resources, cluster together in low-income immigrant enclaves for economic and social reasons. As they gain economic resources, they convert these resources into higher quality housing in neighbourhoods with more and better amenities. Since the non-immigrant majority tend to dominate these neighbourhoods, the move to better housing is usually associated with exiting their ethnic neighbourhood. Ethnic neighbourhoods are seen as a stepping stone and are left behind by longer term migrants once they acquire the requisite financial resources, language and social skills to navigate the larger society.

Where the old immigrant waves were often selected from the most disadvantaged sectors of European society, present day immigrants from the developing world are often selected for their high levels of education and occupational skills. These new immigrants have more housing and neighbourhood options and they are more likely to want both a high quality neighbourhood and a culturally homogenous environment. They are less likely to see that that they have to assimilate into white-dominated neighbourhoods to be 'successful' Canadians, but look to acculturate – combining the best of who they are with the best of what is here.[13]

This transfers into the workplace in that these same immigrants wish to maintain as much of themselves as possible, while at the same time fitting into the new workplace and 'norms' of their organization.

Language and cultural shock

In the television show "Amazing Race", American teams of two race around the world, following clues and completing tasks that explore the local culture and customs. From Rio to Oslo, watching the show has been a great armchair adventure. What is amazing to note are the reactions of the adventurers as they come face to face with culture shock and language issues. As they try to communicate through different languages, accents and language patterns, the frustration is apparent as well as the effect of wrong information received due to misunderstanding.

Immigrants are faced with the workplace's response to their accents every day. In our workplaces, how motivated are the people to work through language issues?

When I go with my mother to see her oncologist, I am highly motivated to work through the language issues I have with her doctor. I need to understand what he is saying because in her situation it really is a case of life or death.

In the workplace, if I have a language issue with a co-worker, I can take a 'pass' on that person, and hope to find the information elsewhere. This could mean delays or incorrect information, but I may feel that it is easier than struggling to make myself understood or to understand.

This can result in the other person feeling irrelevant and soon may withdraw from the work team. It could also lead to toxic work groups where people align with those they can communicate with the best.

Immigrants may find their accent or emphasis on certain syllables to be a source of humour for colleagues, stressing their feeling of being 'other'. In the early 1980's, I worked in the marketing department for a Fortune 100 company in the United States. As the only Canadian in the group of 80 employees in the branch, I quickly worked on my 'abouts' and remembered to say 'vacation' instead of 'holiday'. The feeling of being other was often overwhelming, even in a country where language and much of my home culture was similar. How different would it be where the languages were different?

Old grievances

Just as we do, immigrants bring who they are and their history into the workplace. Some of our own histories can be angry and tragic. We often suggest that this is a new country and that they should 'get over it'. But historical grievances can't be 'gotten over' – they must be 'worked through'. Working through tragic or conflict ridden history does not mean forgetting the past but rather superceding it with something more alive, a form of remembrance that permits progress to be made. Despite the fact that present generations often had little to do with the events in question, they must still confront the past and acknowledge the actions of their nation or group, and victims must let go of their sense of humiliation and "victimhood". If we see ourselves as victims, we hold on to the nastiest pieces of history. When we are put in the place of the aggressor, we wish to minimize the nastiest pieces and justify our actions.

For example, Quebec's vision of history is focused on past episodes where French Quebecers were victims of injustice and unfair treatment (the Acadian deportation, the unsuccessful attempt to annihilate the French language and culture through assimilation). The historical recall in English Canada puts less emphasis on these events and portrays Quebec historically as a spoilt child, fickle and never satisfied.

Canadian historian, Daniel Francis, describes how English Canada shaped our version of who French Canadians were and how they perceived the conquest of the British in the Battle of Quebec.

"For generations, while Quebec historians characterized the Battle of Quebec as a catastrophe, English-Canadian historians described it as a liberation. The conquest was a victory for French colonists because it rescued them from the despotic control of the French monarchy. Canada went from being a neglected economically backward, politically oppressed backwater to a prosperous, progressive member of the British Empire. Who could complain about that? In some school books, "It was a happy time for the French Canadian. They made the delightful discovery that the British, whom they had feared as terrible enemies were really excellent fellows."[14]

Some history and school texts actually presented the Battle of Quebec as a symbol of unity "a bond which now holds French and English united in a Canadian nation"; there are no victors and no vanquished. In this view the conquest was a favour done by the British for which the Quebecois are eternally grateful.

Reconciling the divergent views of Canadian history is made more difficult by the fact that it tends to read in shades of grey rather than in black and white. But understanding the genesis of each side's point of view and acknowledging the errors and grievances that are buried there can help diffuse accumulated frustrations. Historical events taken individually can appear remote from the present day or benign in their current ramifications but their accumulation explains how a relationship can deadlock. In the climate of English and French Canada, the burden of history is one of the major obstacles. Both sides filter actual events through the lens of conflicting perceptions built up over time and their respective mythologies cloud future outcomes.

For many Canadians of European background, we have the luxury of time and space between our lives and the old wars and disagreements of the old country. But for some new Canadians the pain is as fresh as a new wound and the anger as hot as a moment ago. When there are two people in the workplace from opposite sides of a conflict from the other side of the world, it can be difficult to work together. To a third generation Canadian, this seems odd. But to someone who has lived through war or conflict, it is reasonable.

Globalization

What happens around the world impacts our workplace. An immigrant in Canada can be held responsible or be seen as a spokesperson or carrier for issues on the other side of the world.

In the spring of 2003, my husband and I travelled from Hong Kong to Macao for the day. As we disembarked, we walked through a scanner to measure body temperature and possible fever. Although I was tempted to joke with my husband about the possibility of peri-menopausal women registering a higher temperature, the guards at the border wore very serious expressions. SARS was a very serious matter.

"Over 2000 cases identified in more than a dozen countries. More than 80 deaths with China and neighbouring countries hit the worst. Seven SARS deaths in Canada. The Italian doctor who first warned the world about SARS was killed by it. And, as documented by every Canadian newspaper and broadcast, the disease arrived with people who had been in Asia."[15]

If we got on a bus in Toronto in the spring of 2003, there might have been more empty seats beside people who were Asian. SARS originated in the far east and most of those affected with it in the beginning of the outbreak were Asian. The subtle inference was to stay away from open bus seats next to someone who was oriental looking, don't go for coffee with any Chinese co-workers, and certainly don't spend time in any shared enclosed spaces.

Education and credentials

The 2001 Canadian census showed that a gap in labour market conditions persisted between immigrants who landed between 1996 and 2000 and the Canadian-born population. In 2001, 65.8% of recent immigrants aged 25 to 44 were employed, compared with 81.8% of Canadian-born people in the same age group. The unemployment rate of recent immigrants (12.1%) was still nearly twice that of the Canadian-born population (6.4%).

Much of the new talent brought by visible minorities is underutilized because we do not adequately recognize academic or professional credentials obtained abroad. The cost of this failure amounts to between $2 billion and $3 billion annually.[16]

Visible minorities, while often spoken about as one category of employee, are not a homogeneous group. Their realities, their experiences and their opportunities differ. For example, compared with other groups, Blacks, Latin Americans and Filipinos are less likely to be represented in management and scientific positions, while the proportion of Asians holding such positions is greater.

Canada and Canadian organizations continue to under-utilize the skills and talents of new immigrants, 73% of whom were visible minorities in 2003. According to one Statistics Canada study, 6 in 10 immigrants in 2001 did not work in the occupational field in which they had worked prior to arriving in Canada. For most this meant working in sales and service occupations, as well as in those related to processing and manufacturing. Prior to arrival in Canada, the two most common occupational categories for men were natural and applied sciences and management. For women, these categories were business, finance and administration, as well as social science, education, government services and religious occupations.[17]

However, place of birth – and presumably country of origin and minority group status – mattered. Over 60% of immigrants born in the United States, Australia and New Zealand were employed in the same occupational groupings that they had left. In contrast, only 1/3 of those born in Asia and the Middle East were so employed. The figure was 36% for immigrants born in Central and South America.

For the immigrants in this Statistics Canada study, two major hurdles to achieving an occupational fit were difficulty in transferring their qualifications and the lack of Canadian work experience. Virtually all of the immigrant visible minorities who participated in a Conference Board's focus groups (particularly those who immigrated in the skilled workers' stream) were attracted by the promise of rewarding employment opportunities and a high quality of life for themselves and their families. It often takes many years for newcomers to realize their dreams, and for some the prize remains elusive. The view of one focus group participant speaks to the frustration of many: "I had the feeling that I was good enough for immigration, but not good enough for Canadian employers... If Canada needs cab drivers, then Canada should get cab drivers, not professionals."[18]

On a trip to British Columbia, I hiked into a quiet spot below the Bugaboo Glacier. The river was glacier cold but clear and the forest eerily quiet. In the river, young Kokanee salmon with their grey noses and shiny red bodies struggled against the river current. Some would fall back and swim behind other fish to gain rest for the next attempt. Being an immigrant, in the past and today, is rather like that salmon. Part of me wanted to tell them of the problems ahead. Part of me just admired them.

Immigrants to Canada are faced with obstacles to success. As employers, managers and co-workers we can be aware of these issues and assist newcomers in being more successful, and by default, assist our teams and companies in being more successful as well.

ENDNOTES

1. "Census of Population: Labour force activity, occupation, industry, class of worker, place of work, mode of transportation, language of work and unpaid work", *The Daily*, Tuesday, February 11, 2003 Statistics Canada Website.

2. "Vinland, Vinland" Evan Connell, *The White Lantern*, 1979.
Viking Discovery: L'Anse aux Meadows, Joan Horwood, St John's, Newfoundland 1985.

3. Dr. Helge Ingstad found at L'Anse aux Meadows in Newfoundland traces of iron nails, a bronze pin, soapstone spindle whorl of the type used in AD 1000 Iceland.

4. *Canada – A People's History*, Don Gillmore and Pierre Turgeon, 2000.

5. This was further strengthened with a Spanish-Portuguese treaty, *the Treaty of Tordesillas*, a year later.

6. "Bull" as in the second definition meaning "An official and authoritative document issued by the Pope, usually an edict, decree or other proclamation sealed with a bulla (official seal), not as in the first definition of the meaning "1.6 – empty talk or nonsense". (*Funk & Wagnalls Canadian College Dictionary*).

7. "Land of the King of Portugal", *The Beaver – The Magazine of Canada's National History Society*, December 2002/January 2003.

8. *"Outcasts No Longer"*, *Maclean's Magazine*, August 2, 2004.
"The Amazing Grace of the Acadians",*The Beaver*, June, July 2005.

9. *From Slavery to the Ghetto, the Story of the Negro in the Maritimes*, H.A.J. Wedderburn.
Beneath the Clouds of the Promised Land-The Survival of Nova Scotia's Blacks Vol. 1, 1600 -1800, Pachai Bridglal.

10. One of the most famous Canadians to be interned was David Suzuki. Suzuki was born in Vancouver, B.C. in 1936. In 1942 the Suzuki family was sent to an internment camp for the three years. After the war, they were relocated to Ontario. *CBC – The Greatest Canadian*, *www.cbc.ca*.

11. "Canada: Global Citizen", *Canadian Geographic*, Nov/Dec 2004.

12. "Immigration – How does the issue of immigration affect the Canadian Economy and us as Canadians?" and "Immigrant workers needed as Canada ages", Goodale says. Canadian Finance Ralph Goodale spoke about the need for more skilled immigrants to come to Canada at the G7 (France, Germany,

US, Japan, Canada, Italy, Britain) meetings in April 2004 in New York. *Regina Leader Post*, April 24, 2004.

13. "Changing Colours: Spatial Assimilation and New Racial Minority Immigrants", *Canadian Journal Of Sociology*, Winter 2004.

14. *National Dreams: Myth, Memory and Canadian History*, Daniel Francis,1999.

15. "The Racist Face of SARS", *Maclean's*, April 14, 2003.

16. "Brain Gain – The Economic Benefits of Recognizing Learning and Learning Credentials in Canada", Based on data from Michael Bloom and Michael Grant, The Conference Board of Canada, 2001.

17. "Ethnic Diversity Survey: portrait of a multicultural society" Catalogue No. 89-593-XIE, Statistics Canada, September 2003.

18. "Demographic Report for Public Service of Canada by Visible Minorities," Government of Canada, *2002 Public Service Employee Survey: The Results* [on-line] cited May 14, 2004. Available at *www.survey-sondage.gc.ca/2002 Longitudinal Survey of Immigrants to Canada: Process, Progress and Prospects*, Statistics Canada, (2003).

Toward Maximizing the Talents of Visible Minorities: Potential, Performance and Organizational Practices, Judith L. MacBride-King and Prem Benimadhu.

Visible minority population, by provinces and territories (2001 Census)

	Canada	QC	ON	MB	SK
Total population	**29,639,035**	**7,125,580**	**11,285,550**	**1,103,695**	**963,150**
Total visible minority pop.	3,983,845	497,975	2,153,045	87,110	27,580
Black	662,210	152,195	411,095	12,820	4,165
South Asian	917,075	59,505	554,870	12,880	4,090
Chinese	1,029,395	56,830	481,505	11,930	8,085
Korean	100,660	4,410	53,955	1,040	635
Japanese	73,315	2,830	24,925	1,665	435
Southeast Asian	198,880	44,115	86,410	5,480	2,600
Filipino	308,575	18,550	156,515	30,490	3,030
Arab/West Asian	303,965	85,760	155,645	2,100	1,475
Latin American	216,975	59,520	106,835	4,775	2,005
Visible minority not included elsewhere	98,920	7,555	78,915	2,070	420
Multiple visible minority	73,875	6,705	42,375	1,860	640

	AB	BC	YT	NL	PEI
Total population	**2,941,150**	**3,868,870**	**28,520**	**508,075**	**133,385**
Total visible minority pop.	329,925	836,440	1,025	3,850	1,180
Black	31,390	25,465	115	840	370
South Asian	69,585	210,295	210	1,005	115
Chinese	99,095	365,485	225	925	205
Korean	7,800	31,965	0	105	20
Japanese	9,950	32,730	35	70	80
Southeast Asian	23,740	34,970	105	120	45
Filipino	33,940	64,005	235	260	40
Arab/West Asian	24,550	28,985	30	350	180
Latin American	18,745	23,880	45	85	75
Visible minority not included elsewhere	4,220	4,195	10	45	30
Multiple visible minority	6,910	14,465	15	45	20

	NS	NB	N.W.T.	Nvt.	
Total population	**897,570**	**719,710**	**37,105**	**26,665**	
Total visible minority pop.	34,525	9,425	1,545	210	
Black	19,670	3,850	170	65	
South Asian	2,890	1,415	190	30	
Chinese	3,290	1,530	255	35	
Korean	585	105	20	10	
Japanese	420	130	40	0	
Southeast Asian	790	305	190	10	
Filipino	655	355	465	35	
Arab/West Asian	4,000	770	105	15	
Latin American	520	425	55	10	
Visible minority not included elsewhere	1,170	265	20	0	
Multiple visible minority	535	275	35	0	

Source: Statistics Canada, Census of Population. Last modified: 2005-01-25.

Visible minority population, by census metropolitan areas (2001 Census)

	Toronto	Winnipeg	Saskatoon	Vancouver
Total population	**4,647,960**	**661,725**	**222,635**	**1,967,480**
Total visible minority population	1,712,535	82,565	12,410	725,655
Black	310,500	11,440	1,520	18,405
South Asian	473,805	12,285	1,850	164,360
Chinese	409,530	10,930	3,960	342,665
Korean	42,615	955	185	28,850
Japanese	17,415	1,585	140	24,025
Southeast Asian	53,565	5,030	1,130	28,465
Filipino	133,680	30,095	1,460	57,025
Arab/West Asian	95,820	1,960	825	27,330
Latin American	75,910	4,550	845	18,715
Visible minority not included elsewhere	66,455	1,990	175	3,320
Multiple visible minority	33,240	1,745	320	12,495

Source: Statistics Canada, Census of Population. Last modified: 2005-01-25.

Population by mother tongue (2001 Census)

Canada	Total Population	29,639,035
	English	17,352,315
	French	6,703,325
	Chinese	853,745
	Cantonese (Chinese)	322,315
	Mandarin (Chinese)	101,790
	Hakka (Chinese)	4,565
	Chinese, not otherwise stated	425,085
	Italian	469,485
	German	438,080
	Polish	208,375
	Spanish	245,495
	Portuguese	213,815
	Punjabi	271,220
	Ukrainian	148,085
	Arabic	199,940
	Dutch	128,670
	Tagalog (Pilipino)	174,060
	Greek	120,360
	Vietnamese	122,055
	Cree	72,885
	Inuktitut (Eskimo)	29,010
	Other non-official languages	1,506,965

Source: Statistics Canada, Census of Population. Last modified: 2005-01-27.

Population and growth components (1851-2001 Censuses)

Period	Census population at the end of period	Total Population Growth	Births	Deaths	Immigration	Emmigration
	Thousands					
1851-1861	3,230	793	1,281	670	352	170
1861-1871	3,689	459	1,370	760	260	410
1871-1881	4,325	636	1,480	790	350	404
1881-1891	4,833	508	1,524	870	680	826
1891-1901	5,371	538	1,548	880	250	380
1901-1911	7,207	1,836	1,925	900	1,550	740
1911-1921	8,788	1,581	2,340	1,070	1,400	1,089
1921-1931	10,377	1,589	2,415	1,055	1,200	970
1931-1941	11,507	1,130	2,294	1,072	149	241
1941-1951	13,648	2,141	3,186	1,214	548	379
1951-1956	16,081	2,433	2,106	633	783	185
1956-1961	18,238	2,157	2,362	687	760	278
1961-1966	20,015	1,777	2,249	731	539	280
1966-1971	21,568	1,553	1,856	766	890	427
1971-1976	23,450	1,488	1,760	824	1,053	358
1976-1981	24,820	1,371	1,820	843	771	278
1981-1986	26,101	1,281	1,872	885	678	278
1986-1991	28,031	1,930	1,933	946	1,164	213
1991-1996	29,611	1,580	1,936	1,024	1,118	338
1996-2001	31,021	1,410	1,705	1,089	1,217	376

Source: Statistics Canada, Census of Population. Last modified: 2005-01-28.

Immigrant population by place of birth (2001 Census)

Canada	
Total – Place of birth	**5,448,480**
United States	237,920
Central and South America	304,650
Caribbean and Bermuda	294,050
United Kingdom	606,000
Other Northern and Western Europe	494,825
Eastern Europe	471,365
Southern Europe	715,370
Africa	282,600
West Central Asia and the Middle East	285,585
Eastern Asia	730,600
South East Asia	469,105
Southern Asia	503,895
Oceania and other countries	52,525

Source: Statistics Canada, Census of Population. Last modified: 2005-01-26.

CHAPTER NINE
My Kind of Christian?

Recently, at a funeral for a friend who died of breast cancer, I had the opportunity to take a moment to think about my faith. The service was performed at the Holy Rosary Roman Catholic Cathedral. The songs were familiar and I sang each one, the bible verses familiar and I nodded along. I felt comforted and included.

After the ceremony, several people went to the side to light a candle for our friend. Not being Roman Catholic, I didn't know if this was a requirement passed down from the Pope or a cultural tradition. As a non-Catholic sitting in the magnificence of the Cathedral, I not only saw the similarities between my faith and the faith of my friend, but I also mentally registered and judged those practices and traditions that were different.

Many traditions and practices that separate faiths or even denominations within the Christian community set us up for confusion and judgment. As we go along with our own coloured glasses, different for every faith and sect, we judge those who don't behave or believe as we do, referring to them as not "true" Muslims, "good" Christians, or "faithful or sincere" followers. We may judge their faiths as being dogma ridden or radical.

Whether you call it faith or religion, we all belief in something. One who claims to be a skeptic of one set of beliefs is actually a true believer of another set of beliefs.

Our beliefs all begin with some claim about God. What we believe about God affects everything else that we believe and addresses the big questions of life:

⊙ Where did we come from? (origin)

⊙ Who are we? (identity)

⊙ Why are we here? (meaning)

⊙ How should we live? (morality)

⊙ Where are we going? (destiny)

Our beliefs about God usually fall into one of three categories: theism, pantheism or atheism.

- Theism or the idea that "God made everything but is not part of what he made" is where Judaism, Christianity and Islam fall.

- Pantheism or the idea that "God is part of everything he or she made" is where Zen Buddhism, native spirituality and Hinduism reside.

- Atheism or the idea that "there is no God at all" is where atheists and some humanists line up.

- Agnostics are not concerned about religion or don't believe we can really know.

"Despite its apparent persuasiveness, the claim that religion is simply a matter of faith is nothing more than a modern myth – it is just not true. While religion certainly requires faith, religion is not only about faith. Facts are also central to all religions because all religions worldviews – including atheism – make truth claims and many of those truth claims can be evaluated through scientific and historical investigation."[1]

I Don't Have Enough Faith to Be An Athiest, Norman L. Geisler, Frank Turek.

We require faith because as limited human beings, we do not possess the type of knowledge that will provide us with absolute proof of God's existence or non existence and His plans. Outside of the knowledge of our own existence, we deal in the realm of probability. Whatever we've concluded about the existence of God, it is always possible that the opposite conclusion is true. Based on our knowledge, we make an educated guess.

The more rich in diversity our workplace becomes, the more we must be able to defend our personal faith knowledgeably and without anger or hostility. If we investigate and question how we see the world from a religious perspective instead of following our faith blindly, we become strong believers with useful responses to those who ask us about our faith. As our workplace includes more people from various religious beliefs, it becomes more important to be able to see questions not as intolerance but as curiosity and to defend our beliefs in a rational and faith-based way.

We sometimes think that if we are strong believers we should not challenge our faith nor learn about the faith of others, but knowledge and faith go hand in hand, not in opposite directions.

Let's explore the diversity of faiths prominent in Canada, and how conflict among these different belief systems create ongoing issues in the workplace.

Who are the theists who believe that God made everything but is not part of what he made?

Jews worship one God who created the world, is present everywhere and listens to their prayers. They believe they have a special relationship with God which dates back to the times of Abraham. This covenant declares that if Abraham and his people worship God, their descendants would become God's chosen people and live in the promised land of Canaan (now Israel).

Judaism today exists in four forms: orthodox, conservative, reform and messianic.

Orthodox Jews try to follow the letter of the Hebrew law, carefully study the *Torah* (the first five books of the Old Testament) and observe other teachings of respected rabbis that have been added through the centuries, such as the *Mishnah* and the *Talmud*.

These three books (*Torah, Mishnah and Talmud*) rule every facet of the Orthodox Jew's life. For example, the Law of Moses (*Torah*) forbids eating shellfish and pork. Orthodox Jews, as well, will not work, travel, use the phone, write or touch money on the Sabbath.

Synagogues are Jewish houses of worship primarily for prayer and listening to readings from the *Torah*, but also act as centres for study, celebration and socializing. In Orthodox synagogues, men and women worship separately and the service is held in Hebrew.

Conservative Jews have a more lenient interpretation of the *Torah* but they believe the Law is extremely important. They also want to keep the Hebrew language alive and maintain the traditions of Judaism.

Reformed Jews teach that the principles of Judaism are more important that the practices. Most Reformed Jews do not observe the dietary laws or laws constricting every day life, such as what you can or cannot do on the Sabbath.

The Sabbath (or holy day), which all Jews consider important and must be observed, begins at sundown on Friday night and continues until sundown on Saturday. The high holy days of Judaism are Rosh Hashanah (Jewish New Year) and Yom Kippur (Jewish Day of Atonement) which is 10 days later. During this 10-day period, Jews take part in repentance and soul searching. Passover (lasting eight days) celebrates the escape of the Jewish people from slavery in Egypt and is another very important holiday for Jews.

Messianic Jews could go under the Judaism column or the Christian column. Is a Jew no longer a Jew if he accepts Jesus as the son of God?

"Thoughtful Christians are recognizing that the messiahship of Jesus does not necessitate a rejection of all things Jewish. Indeed, the original Jesus movement was entirely Jewish in demographics and outlook. Messianic Jews invoke this early Jesus movement as the model of our community. We seek a new, positive relationship between Judaism and Christianity by providing a living bridge between both."

Russell Resnik, Executive Director, Union of Messianic Jewish Congregations.[2]

Christians are followers of Jesus Christ, a preacher and a teacher who lived over 2000 years ago in Palestine. Jesus was born and raised a Jew and gained supporters among ordinary Jews by performing miracles and teaching forgiveness, but the Jewish authorities disapproved and plotted his downfall.

Christians believe that in the last week of his life, Jesus went to Jerusalem for the Jewish feast of Passover. He was arrested while praying in the Garden of Gethsemane and charged with blasphemy. He was nailed to a cross to die. Three days after his death, his disciples found his tomb empty. Christians believe that Jesus rose from the dead and over the following 40 days, he appeared to his disciples several times before ascending to heaven.

The Holy Scriptures of Christianity are found in *the Bible* (a collection of books comprised of *the Old Testament* containing the Jewish scriptures and *the New Testament* which was written by Christians in the years after Jesus' death). *The New Testament* contains four accounts of Jesus' teaching and life known as the Gospels as well as acts of his disciples. Christians believe the Christian Bible reveals not only God's will but also how Christians should live their lives.

In the centuries following his death, his disciples spread his message. Christians believe that Jesus was the Christ, or 'anointed' one and that, although he lived a human life, he was the Son of God – God in human form. By giving up his own life, he paid the price for human sin. In rising from the dead, he gave people the chance to know God and to experience God's love and forgiveness.

Christians believe in one God, but refer to three aspects of God – God the Father (creator of everything), God the Son (Jesus) and God the Holy Spirit (God's presence in the world and in our lives). This is known as the Holy Trinity.

Christian special events are individual such as baptism or confirmation or are celebrations of events of Jesus' life. These include: communion (recalls the last supper where Jesus asked his disciples to remember him), Christmas (when Christ was born), Epiphany (visit of three wise men to the infant Jesus), Lent (40 days before Easter when Christians remember their sins to commemorate the 40 days and nights Jesus spent fasting and praying in the desert), Holy week (the week before Easter), Good Friday (the day Jesus died), Easter Sunday (to celebrate Jesus' rising from the dead), Feast of the Ascension (Thursday 40 days after Easter Sunday the day on which Jesus ascended into heaven), Pentecost (celebration of God sending down the Holy Spirit to Jesus' disciples whereby they could speak in different languages so that they could spread the good news of Christ).

Sunday is the Sabbath day for Christians as this was the day they believe that Jesus rose from the dead.

Most Christians share the same basic beliefs, but there are many ways of expressing them. The three main groups are: Orthodox, Roman Catholic and Protestant. What separated Christians into these main groups were disagreements over authority (who is the true church with the exclusive right and ability to interpret the word of God), and salvation (how a person finds justification from his or her sins).

Roman Catholics or 'Catholics' represent the largest Christian community with close to 1 billion members worldwide, and 13 million in Canada.3 In regards to authority, according to the 'Catechism of the Catholic Church', Jesus named his apostle, Peter, as the spiritual leader with cardinals and bishops as the administrative arm guiding and ministering in various geographical locations around the world.

Catholics believe that scripture and 'sacred' tradition' are equal in authority and that the teaching authority of the Roman Church has been entrusted to interpret the Bible in order to provide one common belief for all. Catholics believe that Peter was the first pope and that through apostolic succession4 other popes have succeeded him, each serving as 'vicar of Christ'. Catholics also believe that the pope is infallible when he speaks 'ex cathedra' (meaning from the chair or with 'authority') on matters of faith and morals.

In regards to salvation, Catholics believe that salvation is secured by two things: faith in Christ as their saviour and good works.

Orthodox believers are not 'just like the Catholics but without a pope'. There are at least 13 different independent and self governing churches, 200 million Orthodox Christians worldwide and 500,000 in Canada.

Many people are confused by the many Orthodoxies that are grouped under the one term "Orthodox". This goes back to the very reason for the split between the Orthodox Patriarch of Constantinople and the Bishop of Rome (the Pope) in 1054. For Orthodox Christians, each region of the map should have its own head or patriarch and he should control what happens under his jurisdiction; he should not be subjected to a higher church authority. From the beginning, there were four Patriarchates: Constantinople, Alexandria, Antioch and Jerusalem. Eleven others were added: Russia, Romania, Serbia, Greece, Georgia, Bulgaria, Cyprus, Czechoslovakia, Poland, Albania and Sinai. Each of these church bodies is independent of each other. Each is governed by a bishop and have equal weight to the other, even though much of orthodox tradition and teaching has been shaped by the first four.

There are many groups of **Protestant** Christians (such as Baptists, Lutherans, Methodists, Episcopalians, Presbyterians, United Church of Christ, Quakers, Mennonites, and Pentecostals) but there are some common elements in the question of authority and salvation.

Sola scriptura means the Bible alone is all that is needed for spiritual authority. All the things a Christian needs to know, believe and practice are clearly stated in the scriptures which are given by inspiration of God.

Sola fide means faith alone is the source of salvation. Faith yields good works and salvation, versus good works and faith yielding salvation.

Islam began 1400 years ago in the city of Mecca in western Arabia (now Saudi Arabia) when the prophet Muhammad began proclaiming the message. That message is "there is only one God". Muslims, the followers of Muhammad believe that Muhammad was the last in a series of prophets through which Allah (God) revealed his wishes for the world. The previous prophets included Moses, Noah, and Jesus.

The word Islam comes from the word 'submission' in Arabic, and Muslims are people who submit to Allah's will and try to live in a way that is pleasing to Allah.

The Holy book of Muslims is the *Qur'an* (Quran or Koran) and is believed to contain the perfect word of Allah as revealed to Muhammad through the angel Gabriel. The *Qur'an* tells Muslims how to worship, how to treat other people, what to eat and wear, and how to live a good life. Muslims believe that the *Qur'an* has always existed in heaven, written in Arabic on a tablet of stone.

The five central beliefs of Islam are called the Five Pillars of Islam and are:

1. – Shahada, the first pillar, is a statement of faith – "There is no god but Allah and Muhammad is his prophet" or "There is no god but Allah and Muhammad is his messenger".

2. – Salat, the second pillar, is prayer. The obligatory prayers are said five times a day and are considered a direct link between the worshipper and God. There is no hierarchical authority in Islam, and no priests, so the prayers are led by a learned person who knows *the Qur'an*, chosen by the congregation. The five prayers contain verses from *the Qur'an* and are said in Arabic. Prayers are said at dawn, noon, mid-afternoon, sunset and nightfall. Muslims can pray anywhere.

Chapter (Sura) One of the *Koran* is the prayer that is used five times a day in the life of a Muslim. It reads:

In the name of God
The Compassionate
The Merciful
Praise be to God, Lord of the Universe,
The Compassionate, the Merciful,
Sovereign of the Day of Judgment!
You alone we worship,
and to You alone we turn for help
Guide us to the straight path
The path of those whom you have favoured,
Not of those who have incurred Your wrath,
*Nor of those who have gone astray.*5

3. – Zakat, or the giving of alms to the poor and needy, is the third pillar. All things belong to God, and that wealth is therefore held in trust by humans. Zakat means growth and purification. Our possessions are purified by setting aside a portion for those in need.

4. – Sawm, the fourth pillar, requires Muslims to fast during the holy month of Ramadan. From first light to sundown, Muslims abstain from food, drink and sexual relations.

5. – Hajj, the fifth and final pillar, is the pilgrimage to Makkah (Mecca) which all Muslims hope to perform at least once during their lifetime. It is an obligation only for those who are physically and financially able. The Hajj begins in the 12th month of the Islamic year (which is lunar not solar) and closes with the festival, the Eid al-Adha celebrated with prayers and exchange of gifts. This and the Eid al-Fitr (a feast day commemorating the end of Ramadan) are the main festivals of the Muslim calendar.

Friday is the Muslim holy day and the only day on which men must go to the mosque to pray. Women may attend Friday but it is not required. They can pray at home. Both male and female Muslims avoid pork and alcohol.

In the 7th and 8th centuries following Muhammad's death, the Islamic faith spread rapidly through Arabia and neighboring countries. This was due to Muslim traders and to the expansion by Muslim armies establishing a vast empire from Spain and North Africa to India. Today more than 20% of the world is Muslim and over 600,000 Canadians are as well.

Who are the Pantheists who believe that God is part of everything he made?

Hinduism is one of the world's oldest and most varied religions with some 700 million followers worldwide and 300,000 in Canada. Hindus usually do not use the word 'Hinduism' to describe their religion; they use the term *sanatana dharma* meaning the 'eternal law'.

Hinduism dates back more than 4000 years to the time of the great Indus Valley civilization in the Indian subcontinent. Around 2000 BCE the nomadic Aryan people came over the Caucasus mountains and invaded what is now India. Their religious ideas mixed with those of the people of the Indus valley to form the basis of Hinduism as it is practiced today.

Most Hindus believe in a supreme soul or spirit without form called Brahman. Many Hindu gods and goddesses represent the different aspects of Brahman's power and character. The three main gods are Brahma (the creator), Vishnu (the preserver or protector) and Shiva (the destroyer). Hindus may worship one god, many gods or none at all. Most Hindus, in addition to the three main gods, worship other gods and goddesses such as Rama and Krishna. Both are incarnations of the god Vishnu. Hindus believe that Vishnu appeared on earth many times to save the world from disaster but he was always in disguise. Hindu deities are a mixture of good and evil, kindness and cruelty. For example, Parvati, the wife of Shiva is worshiped both as the kind mother goddess and the blood-thirsty goddess of war.

There are no set rules for being a Hindu. One can be a good Hindu and believe in one god, many gods or no gods at all. For Hindus, these contradictory ideas are not seen as a problem. There are, however, two fundamental beliefs that all Hindus share: reincarnation and *karma*.

Reincarnation is the belief that a person's uncreated and eternal soul must repeatedly be recycled into the world in different bodies. In some forms of Hinduism, souls may be reincarnated as animals, plants or even inanimate objects. Reincarnation is the process that takes the Hindu through *samsara*, the many lives that each soul must endure before reaching *moksha* where it is liberated from suffering and becomes one with the infinite Brahman.

Who or what you are reborn as depends on your actions in your previous life. This process is known as *karma*. If you lead a good life, you will have a better rebirth and move closer to *moksha*. Hinduism teaches that the soul is perfect, free and unlimited and no matter how many lives are required, eventually each and every soul will reach its divine nature. There are three paths to *moksha*: the path of works or *dharma*, the path of knowledge or *inana*, or the path of passionate devotion or *bhakti*.

Many Hindus worship in temples. Each temple, or *mandir*, is dedicated to a particular god or goddess and is believed to be the deity's earthly home. There are no set times or days to go to the temple. Some Hindus also set aside a place in their home as a shrine, which could be a small space for a statue or a picture.

When Hindus visit the temple they usually take off their shoes and women cover their heads as a sign of respect. Hindus visit a temple to pray and to view the statue representing the deity. They may take offerings of fruit, flowers or incense. These gifts are called *prasad*. The priest presents the gifts to be blessed, returns them to the worshipers and marks their foreheads with a red mark of blessing. This ceremony is known as *puja*.

The oldest Hindu sacred texts are the four collections of hymns, prayers and stories called the *Vedas* which were composed over 3000 years ago. Other important texts include the *Upanishads* and two long poems called the *Mahabharata* and the *Ramayana*. The *Upanishads* are teachings presented in the form of stories and parables.

There are many Hindu festivals to mark special occasions such as birthdays of the gods and goddesses, harvest time and family events. Many Hindus also make pilgrimages to sacred places such as the city of Varanasi on the banks of the Holy River Ganges. Every 12 years in January or February, millions of pilgrims travel to the banks of the River Ganges at Allahabad to celebrate the *Kumbha Mela*.

Most Hindus celebrate the main festivals of the year – Diwali, Holi and Dessehra. These are lively, colorful occasions where people visit the temple, eat special food and exchange candy and gifts. Diwali is the festival of lights (late October or early November), Holi marks the coming of spring (March or April), and Dussehra (September) marks Rama's triumph over the Ravana.

The founder of **Buddhism** was Siddhartha Gautama, a royal prince born in Nepal about 564 BCE. After many years of prayer and meditation, Siddhartha gained enlightenment, meaning he finally understood the basic truths of life. After his enlightenment, Siddhartha spent the rest of his life traveling around India, teaching and preaching. He soon had a loyal band of followers and was given the title Buddha or 'awakened one'.

Buddha did not want to be worshipped as a God. He taught that people would be happier if they took responsibility for their own thoughts and actions. His teachings were simply a guide for living.

The Buddha's enlightenment had shown him that people suffered because they were never happy with what they had and always wanted more. They needed to learn new ways of thinking and behaving, so he set out his basic teachings in the "Four Noble Truths":

1. *Human life is full of suffering*. Even death brings no relief because of reincarnation. Salvation or *nirvana* is to be released from the cycle.

2. *The cause of suffering is greed*. We are too attached to our health, wealth, status and physical comfort. We fall victim to attachment and desire.

3. *There is an end to suffering*. Suffering ends when we cease to crave what we want and cannot have.

4. *The way to end suffering is to follow the middle path*.

The middle path lies between extreme luxury and extreme hardship. It had eight steps that would lead people to live wiser and more compassionate lives:

- Right understanding (of the Buddha's teachings)
- Right attitude (positive thinking)
- Right speech (not telling lies)
- Right action (helping others)
- Right work (doing a useful job)
- Right effort (doing good things)
- Right mindfulness (thinking before you speak or act)
- Right meditation (developing a calm, happy mind).

The five Precepts (or guidelines) that Buddhists follow in daily life are:

- do not harm or kill living things
- do not take things unless they are freely given

- lead a decent life
- do not speak unkindly or lie, and
- do not take drugs or alcohol.

Buddhists believe that sin is the lust that arises in one's life and they seek to rid themselves of lustful desires by self-effort. In some ways, Buddhism is similar to Hinduism from which it evolved. In other ways, it is quite different and many of Buddha's teachings were rejected as heresy by the dominant teachers of Hinduism, the Brahmin priests. Buddha denied that the *Vedas* and *Upanishads* were divine writings. He also denied that man has a soul which is part of the Brahman world soul. Other Hindu concepts Buddha rejected included the Brahmin priesthood and the entire Hindu sacrificial system. He taught that enlightenment was open to anyone including women, not just Brahmin males. Buddha radically challenged all the different Hindu gods and goddesses saying they were unimportant in the quest for enlightenment. Buddha did accept the Hindu teachings on reincarnation, along with *Karma* and *dharma*. Buddha taught that one could be reincarnated as a human being, an animal, an angry ghost, a demon, or a Hindu god. He also incorporated yoga and meditation, which were highly developed skills in Hinduism, directly into his teachings.

Buddhism was popular in India for several centuries until it was absorbed by Hinduism. Brahmin priests even promoted the Buddha to an incarnation of the god of Vishnu. During the first 1000 years CE, Buddhist monks spread Buddhism throughout the Orient. There are three main kinds: Theravada, Mahayana and Tantrism.

In **Theravada,** or 'way of the elders', only a fortunate few lifelong monks can find *nirvana* by absolutely following the way of Buddha. The best that laypeople could hope for in Theravada Buddhism was to rise to a higher level when reborn in their next life so they too may become monks.

Mahayana Buddhism, or "the greater way" teaches that Buddha believed that *nirvana* is available to all people. Buddha originally taught that the only person who can save you is you, but Mahayana developed the idea of saviour gods or 'Bodhisattvas'.

Followers of Mahayana believed that Buddha was the first and supreme Bodhisattva or saviour to mankind who can be called on by the faithful. Other Buddhist monks who achieve *nirvana* and become enlightened as Buddha did are also Bodhisattvas. To Theravada Buddhists, Buddha was only a teacher but to Mahayana Buddhists, Buddha has been raised to the position of a saviour god.

Another popular form of Mahayana Buddhism is **Zen**, a discipline with the primary goal of experiencing enlightenment through meditation. Zen teachers emphasize the saying of the Buddha: "Look within, you are the Buddha."

The third major group of Buddhism is **Tantrism**, a blending of Mahayana Buddhism with the ancient occult practices of Tibet. Tantric Buddhism uses incantations and contains elements of animism (attributing conscious life to inanimate objects or objects in nature). Tantrism is considered the official religion of Tibet.

There are more than 400 million Buddhists globally (300,000 in Canada).

As Christianity flowed from Judaism and Islam flowed from both, so has Sikhism flowed from Islam and Hinduism. Each faith took some elements of what went before and yet were faiths individual and distinct in themselves.

Often mistaken as a combination of Hinduism and Islam, the Sikh religion can be characterized as a completely independent faith. Over 20 million Sikhs follow this distinct religion born 500 years ago in the Punjab region of northern India. Between 1469 and 1708, ten Gurus preached a message of truth, devotion to God, and universal equality.

At the time of the birth of Sikhism, the two main religions in India were Hinduism and Islam but there were deep divisions between the two and many people felt excluded. Guru Nanak, a religious teacher introduced the new religion of Sikhism which taught tolerance of the faiths. When Guru Nanak died his teaching was carried on by nine other gurus or teachers ending with Guru Gobind Singh. It is believed that the ten Gurus all had the same soul though they had different bodies, and that it was Guru Nanak's spirit which passed on into his nine successors. While the Sikhs hold their Gurus in high reverence, they are not to be worshipped. Sikhs may worship only God.

Sikhs believe that there is only one god and they try to remember God in everything they do. This task of remembering is closely linked to the idea of service or *seva*. Service involves doing things for others without thinking of your own reward. By practicing these ideals and following the example set by the gurus, Sikhs hope to grow closer to God.

Guru Nanak preached that in God's eyes, everyone is equal. Followers were encouraged to leave their Hindu caste symbols and take on a common surname: all Sikh men took the surname or middle name Singh meaning lion, and all Sikh women took the surname Kaur meaning princess.

Many Sikhs visit a temple or *gurudwara* to pray. When entering the temple, worshipers must take off their shoes and cover their heads as a mark of respect. They bow in front of the Sikh holy book, the *Guru Granth Sahib*, and sit to listen to hymns read from the scriptures by a male or female reader. When Guru Gobind Singh died in 1708, he told the Sikhs that in the future the sacred scriptures should be their new guru. The scriptures collected together in the *Guru Granth Sahib* were devotional hymns composed by six of the gurus and other holy men.

Devout Sikhs have five symbols of faith known as the Five Ks because they each begin with the letter 'k' in the Punjab language: Kesh (uncut hair) symbolizing obedience to God, Kanga (wooden comb) symbolizes cleanliness, Kachcha (shorts worn under clothes) symbolizes goodness, Kara (stainless steel bracelet worn on right wrist) symbolizes eternity, and Kirpan (sword) which symbolizes strength.

A Sikh must observe and follow a strict code of conduct that includes: worshipping only one God, reciting five prescribed hymns everyday, learning the Punjabi language and reading *Guru Granth Sahib*, wearing and observing the significance of five Ks, living a truthful life and treating all humans as equal. He must not cut his body hair, eat kosher meat, smoke, take drugs or intoxicants, or have faith in black magic, superstitions, charms or rituals.

There are about 16 million Sikhs in the world today with 300,000 in Canada.

We mentioned **agnostics** and **atheists** earlier. Until the 19th century, anyone who was an agnostic also was considered to be an atheist or one who believes in no god. It was then that a British Freethinker named Thomas Huxley coined the term agnostic. Since then, much has been debated about what an agnostic is exactly. An agnostic can just be someone who says "I don't know if there is a god" and tries to find out by using logical thinking and scientific fact gathering. But an agnostic can also be someone who says "I can't know" and argues that no matter how good your method or how many facts you produce, you can't know some things – like the nature of God.

One thing we have seen through this chapter is that as different as faiths are from each other, there are also some commonalities. For example, Islam in some ways is very close to Judaism. They agree on much of history, they acknowledge Jesus existed, and they see him not as the son of God, but still as someone very special. Today we are seeing more faiths and denominations trying to bridge their differences and be more inclusive. Consider the recent decision of the Canadian Forces to commission Captain Suleyman Demiray as its first Muslim chaplain on December 10th, 2003. In the past, the chaplaincy that served the forces has been overwhelmingly Christian with 166 regular force and 140 reserve force Christian chaplains. [6] Another example is the coming together of three Christian denominations (Eastside United Church, Bread of Life Lutheran Church and St. Philip Anglican Church) to share facility space in Regina, Saskatchewan.[7]

So then, why can't we just get along?

Ongoing Issues

The requirement of being right

"The central tenet of every religious tradition is that all others are mere repositories of error, or at best, incomplete. Intolerance is thus intrinsic to every creed. Once a person believes – really believes – that certain ideas can lead to eternal happiness, or to its antithesis, he cannot tolerate the possibility that the people he loves might be led astray by the

blandishments of unbelievers. Certainly a certainty about the next life is simply incompatible with tolerance in this one."[8]

Sam Harris

And therein lies the trouble with religious diversity. We are all so certain we are right. We think that our faith is one step up from what has gone before and everything that comes after is heresy. It could be Christians challenging Jewish beliefs, Mormons challenging Protestantism, or Muslims challenging Christianity and Judaism. In *"The Trouble with Islam"*, Canadian writer Irshad Manji discusses this regarding Muslims in Canada.[9]

"Even in the West, Muslims are routinely taught that the Koran is the final manifesto of God's will, displacing the Bible and the Torah. As the final manifesto, it's the 'perfect' scripture – not to be questioned, analyzed or even interpreted, but simply believed. "

Assumption of Sameness

Even how we describe time assumes a Christian focus in our world:

A.D. Anno Domini – In the Year of Our Lord or after the death of Christ
B.C. Before Christ

More and more, as you have seen in this text, we are embracing faith-neutral terms:

C.E. Current Era
B.C.E. Before Current Era

Religious pluralism creates challenges in the workplaces of any multicultural society. Communicating, being flexible and accommodating for individual differences are keys to making a workplace conflict free.

"Creed" is a term defined by the Ontario Human Rights Commission as a "professed system and confession of faith, including both beliefs and observances of worship. A belief in a God or gods, or a single supreme being or deity is not a requisite." The Ontario commission's position is that every person has the right to be free from harassing behaviour that is based on religion or which arises because the person who is the target of the behaviour does not share the same faith. This means that the law can require measures to facilitate the practice of religious observance but also it means that no person can force another to accept or comply with religious beliefs or practices.

We often think this primarily applies to people with strong opposing faiths to the Christian-dominant workplace but it also includes people who some would describe as not having a religion such as atheists and agnostics.

We discussed the range of sub-groups that exist within larger faith groups. At one end of the spectrum are those who practice their faith in a serious and devoted way and at the other end are those who are culturally of one faith but do not practice.

For example, many people raised in a Christian environment may say they are Christian on the Census form but do not practice their faith in a meaningful way through prayer, confession of their sins either directly to God or through an intermediary (as in the Catholic faith), or attend church outside of the days their family applies pressure for them to do so. Because of this traditionalism around Christianity, there is grey area between secular Christian behaviour (Santa Claus, Christmas parties) and celebration of the faith.

This situation leads to an assumption of sameness – that most people in our workplaces are Christian either traditionally or practicing. Therefore it is an easy assumption that Christian-based events will be welcome and appropriate to the entire staff.

The outcome of this perspective is that non-Christians who have strong beliefs in other quarters or non-Christians with atheist or agnostic beliefs will usually feel uncomfortable, excluded, and not respected. They may not even attend. When a more respectful way of doing things is brought up, those planning the events may even reply that if those who don't feel comfortable don't wish to attend, no one is insisting they do. Yet we know that some organizations frown on not attending social events in the workplace.

So my choice then as someone who is atheist, Muslim or Jew is to decide whether not to go and hope there is no negative impact on my career and that no one will judge me as not being a 'team player' or seeing myself 'above socializing with the group'; or, I attend and feel uncomfortable. When we are part of the dominant religious group in the workplace, this is difficult to get our heads around. We wonder what is the big deal and why can't people fit in. But why should someone give up something that is intrinsic to who they are so that the workplace can continue to pretend that its 'agreements' are still working when they really are not?

When I was in Hong Kong, we visited many Buddhist temples. At a particularly magnificent temple, my husband suggested that I play the tourist, buy incense from the temple keeper, light it and put it in the different spots reserved for the different problems a person may be having.

I had two reactions. One was that it was a slippery slope to take for the sake of a fun thing to do. Praying to Buddha would be directly opposed to my religious faith. The second reaction was how disrespectful it would be to sincere devout Buddhists for me to follow the practices of Buddhism simply for the tourist factor.

When I speak at conferences, particularly on diversity, I find the organizers make an effort to have a religiously respectful agenda. In spite of this, our entrenched 'assumed sameness' is evident. The multi-faith service is scheduled on Sunday morning. Not Saturday to align with the Jewish faith, Friday to align with the Muslim faith, but Sunday which is the Christian day of worship. So multi-faith really means multi-denominational and we are just trying to make it look diversity friendly.

ENDNOTES

1. *I Don't Have Enough Faith to Be An Athiest*, Norman L. Geisler, Frank Turek, 2004.

2. Russell Resnik, Executive Director, Union of Messianic Jewish Congregations, as quoted in "Jesus and Jews", *First Things* (Institute on Religion and Public Life), May 2005.

3. Charts of religions in Canada – see following pages.

4. Apostolic succession grew out of the Christian Church's move toward an episcopal type of government in the 1st and 2nd centuries. Bishops became the most important officials and by the late 2nd century were considered the successors to the apostles, complete with their power, authority and wisdom.

5. *The Koran*, Penguin Classics.

6. "First Muslim chaplain to serve Canadian Forces", *National Post*, December 11, 2003.

7. "Historic Christian Unity", *Regina Leader Post*, June 28, 1997.

8. *The End of Faith: Religion, Terror, and the Future of Reason*, Sam Harris.

9. *The Trouble With Islam*, Irshad Manji, 2003.

Population by religion, by provinces and territories (2001 Census)

	Canada	N.L.	P.E.I.	N.S.	N.B.
Total population	**29,639,035**	**508,080**	**133,385**	**897,570**	**719,710**
Catholic	12,936,905	187,440	63,265	328,700	386,050
Protestant	8,654,850	303,195	57,080	438,150	263,075
Christian Orthodox	479,620	365	245	3,580	635
Christian not inc. elsewhere	780,450	2,480	3,205	10,105	8,120
Muslim	579,640	630	195	3,545	1,275
Jewish	329,995	140	55	2,120	670
Buddhist	300,345	185	140	1,730	545
Hindu	297,200	405	30	1,235	475
Sikh	278,410	135	0	270	90
Eastern religions	37,550	110	105	565	330
Other religions	63,975	135	100	1,155	790
No religious affiliation	4,900,090	12,865	8,950	106,405	57,665

	Canada	Que.	Ont.	Man.	Sask.
Total population	**29,639,035**	**7,125,580**	**11,285,550**	**1,103,700**	**963,150**
Catholic	12,936,905	5,939,715	3,911,760	323,690	305,390
Protestant	8,654,850	335,590	3,935,745	475,185	449,195
Christian Orthodox	479,620	100,375	264,055	15,645	14,280
Christian not inc. elsewhere	780,450	56,750	301,935	44,535	27,070
Muslim	579,640	108,620	352,530	5,095	2,230
Jewish	329,995	89,915	190,795	13,040	865
Buddhist	300,345	41,380	128,320	5,745	3,050
Hindu	297,200	24,525	217,555	3,835	1,585
Sikh	278,410	8,225	104,785	5,485	500
Eastern religions	37,550	3,425	17,780	795	780
Other religions	63,975	3,870	18,985	4,780	6,750
No religious affiliation	4,900,090	413,190	1,841,290	205,865	151,455

	Canada	Alta.	B.C.	Y.T.
Total population	**29,639,035**	**2,941,150**	**3,868,875**	**28,520**
Catholic	12,936,905	786,360	675,320	6,015
Protestant	8,654,850	1,145,460	1,213,295	9,485
Christian Orthodox	479,620	44,475	35,655	150
Christian not inc. elsewhere	780,450	123,140	200,345	1,010
Muslim	579,640	49,040	56,220	60
Jewish	329,995	11,085	21,230	35
Buddhist	300,345	33,410	85,540	130
Hindu	297,200	15,965	31,500	10
Sikh	278,410	23,470	135,310	100
Eastern religions	37,550	3,335	9,970	190
Other religions	63,975	10,560	16,205	330
No religious affiliation	4,900,090	694,840	1,388,300	11,015

Source: Statistics Canada, Census of Population. Last modified: 2005-01-25.

CHAPTER TEN
Crossing the Gender Divide

Men and women are together in the workplace, side by side, cubicle by cubicle, day by day. We each represent half of the workforce and yet we can't seem to get along. [1]

Men want to understand why women behave the way they do. Women want to understand men. Sometimes we feel we really are from two different planets.

Men and women are biologically different in many different ways. Society has alternately denied or embraced this truth. When we deny differences exist, men and women are not able to work to their full potential. If we acknowledge a difference without understanding the reason behind it, we make assumptions and risk creating unfounded stereotypes that could also limit success and reduce workplace productivity.

Let's consider the science behind some of our differences and the possible consequences of not understanding those differences.

How we hear

Girls hear better than boys. Teachers in the K-6 levels are most likely to be women, boys are most likely to gravitate to the back of the room and girls to the front. The impact of this is that female teachers who unconsciously speak loud enough for their own comfort are also communicating at a level loud enough for the girls, but not loud enough for the boys. The boys tune out because they are not being drawn in. This can lead to an ADD diagnosis, a Ritalin prescription, being labeled a poor student and being required to work extra time with the teacher or complete more homework to succeed. Our education system sets boys up for failure by not acknowledging this biological diversity.[2]

This may also explain why women may be more distracted by workplace noise and men may not register low level noise.

Compartmentalization

In the late 1800s, French neurologist Charles Edouard Brown-Séquard and British neurologist Henry Charlton Bastian independently discovered that that the left side of the brain is specialized for language. A man who suffers a stroke affecting the left side of the brain is more likely to lose language functions than a man who suffers a stroke on the right side of his brain. The right side of a man's brain seems to be specialized for spatial functions such as navigation or mental imagery.[3]

All tests were done on male patients, and the results extrapolated to conclude that women would experience the same effect. It wasn't until 1964 that someone challenged the 'assumed sameness' of male-only research.

Male and female brains are organized differently with functions more compartmentalized in male brains and more globally distributed in female brains. Men who suffer a stroke affecting the left hemisphere suffer a drop of verbal IQ of about 20% with no drop in verbal IQ if the stroke is on the right side. Women experience a drop of verbal IQ of approximately 9%–11% when they have a stroke on either hemisphere.

By 1985, it was clear that the compartmentalization of function that was so obvious in men's brains did not apply to women.[4]

This compartmentalization data raises two points.

One is that we cannot assume that scientific research performed on men applies equally to women. For example, research has shown that when men cross their arms in front of their chest, they are giving a hint of their resistance or indifference to what is being said. Women are likely to cross their arms in front of them for various reasons that disagree with this male-focused data: nowhere to put their hands due to lack of pockets in women's business suits, a chill in the air, or merely that it is a comfortable pose.[5] When we assume we know why women react the way they do based on evidence of men's reactions in similar situations, we risk miscommunication and conflict.

The second point relates to the difference in the ability to multi-task. If the mind of a female is more globally distributed, this may give her an ability to focus on many things at a time. If a male mind is more compartmentalized it gives him the ability to focus intently on one task at a time. Both of these ways of thinking are valuable, but recognizing our differences regarding not only what skills we are better at but what skills we are naturally good at gives us the opportunity to utilize these differences to create more effective teams in the workplace.

In a recent issue of the international publication, *The Economist*, Chris Clark, CEO of the US headhunting firm Boyden and visiting professor at Henley Management College in Britain, makes an argument that women are superior to men at multi-tasking, team building and communicating, which have become the essential skills for running a 21st century corporation. [6]

Retinal preference

Females are born pre-wired to be interested in faces and males are pre-wired to be interested in moving objects. This leads females to be more relationship focused and males more action focused.

This difference is biologically found in the retina of the male and female eye. The retina has two layers, the second of which is made up of 'P' and 'M' cells. M cells are motion detectors and track objects anywhere in the visual field. They answer the question "Where is it now and where is it going?" 'M' cells compile information about direction and motion. 'M' cells dominate the male retina.

'P' cells focus on the question, "What is it?" They compile data about texture and colour. Female retinas are rich in 'P' cells.[7]

This difference in 'P' and 'M' cells gives women an increased ability over men to identify orange as having many shades from pale peach to vibrant coral, while men are likely to identify orange as 'orange'.

Can you see how this difference may create conflict on your team?

Describing negative emotion

Negative emotions are processed differently in male and female brains. In children, research shows that negative emotional activity in response to unpleasant or disturbing visual images seems to be localized in primitive areas deep in the brain, in the amygdala. If you ask six-year-olds why they are sad, they find it difficult to tell you. This is because the part of the brain where the emotions are happening is not well connected to the part of the brain where verbal processing and speech happens.

In adolescence, a larger fraction of the brain activity associated with negative emotion moves up to the cerebral cortex that is in the same division of the brain associated with other cognitive functions such as reflection and language. So the teenager or young adult is able to better explain why she is feeling sad. But this change only happens in women. For male brains, even in adulthood, the activity associated with negative emotion remains in the amygdala.

The EQ (emotional intelligence) movement that has been sweeping Canada and the US focuses in part on the ability for people to increase their ability to express emotion with those they lead. Men are not brain-wired to feel as comfortable sharing negative feelings as women are. Women are pre-disposed to share negative emotion and men are pre-disposed not to. If our workplace is defined by sharing less, women may be labeled as touchy-feely, too emotional and not businesslike. Men in a more person-focus environment could be labeled emotionless, cold and uncaring.

This is not new to many leaders. Some woman managers see that this can be an advantage for women in the workplace of the future. Maria Wisniewska, who headed a Polish bank, Bank Pekao, and is an international advisor to The Conference Board says, "The links between the rational and emotional parts of the brain are greater in women than in men. If so, and if leadership is about making links between emotion and intelligence, then maybe women are better at it than men."[8]

Are women 'better' at linking emotion and intelligence or is it just more natural for us to do so?

Risk taking

As children, boys enjoy taking risks. Most boys are impressed by other boys who take risks. Especially if the risk-taker succeeds. Girls are less likely to enjoy risk-taking for its own sake and are much less likely to be impressed by risk-taking behaviour in others. Girls may be willing to take risks but they are less likely to seek out risky situations just for the sake of living dangerously.[9]

Part of this difference is that risky and dangerous activities trigger a 'flight or fight' response that gives a tingly charge, an excitement that many boys find irresistible. The increased heart rate, dilated pupils, a surge of adrenaline in the blood preparing them to fight or run away is how men physiologically respond to risky situations.

Women, however, respond to threat and confrontation with the 'puke and pee' response – they feel dizzy, nauseous and need to go to the bathroom frequently. As little individual study has been done on how women specifically respond to threat and stressful situations, we see again that much scientific data is based on male studies extrapolated to include women. [9]

The assertive male risk-taking strategy sometimes works for men and sometimes leads them to over-estimate their ability. For example, nearly all drowning victims are male. Research shows that men consistently overestimate their ability to swim in threatening situations. [10]

Women consistently underestimate their ability and minimize their risk of failure. In her book, *Women Don't Ask: Negotiation and the Gender Divide*, Linda Babcock studied students graduating from Carnegie Mellon University with a Masters degree in a business related field. She found that the starting salaries of the men were about 8% on average higher than those of the women. The men were paid about $4,000 more.

Babcock looked to see who asked for more money during the job finding process. Only 7% of the female students had asked compared with 57% of the male students. Students that asked for more money received a starting salary that was $4,053 higher on average than those who did not ask. The male students were more inclined to take the risk of offending the hiring human resource officer for the sake of a higher starting salary.[11]

On a hourly rate comparison of employed Canadians, women make an average of $16.54 per hour and men make an average of $19.74 per hour. This means that for every $1.00 a man makes, a woman makes $.84. [12] In a Statistics Canada National Graduate Survey, the graduates from year 2000 show that two years later in 2002, the median salary for the female university grads working full time was $37,000 and for men it was $42,000. [13]

Although women's cautious risk-taking strategy mentioned above can justify some of the difference in the gender gap, there are many other reasons holding back women's success.

In a presentation to the Pay Equity Task Force on June 20, 2002, BPW Canada (Canadian Federation of Business and Professional Women's Clubs) argued that the wage gap is due to many factors including higher rate of unionization among men, higher education, seniority levels, women leaving the workforce for home responsibilities that affect continuous service, and gender discrimination.[14]

Relationships in the workplace

Women's friendships are about being together, spending time together, talking together, and going places together. Friendships between men usually develop out of a shared interest in a project, game, or activity.

For example, men might have friends that they golf with, fish with, and coach soccer with. None of these friends or activities cross over. Individual friends for individual activities. Women, however, are more likely to have friends that are included in all their interests. When women are stressed, they want to be with their friends more. When men are stressed, they want to be with their friends less.

Part of this may be due to the fact that women can express their negative emotions with others easier than men and so 'venting' comes more natural and is more therapeutic. Women find self-revelation binds them together and men find self-revelation embarrassing and to be avoided at all costs. Women have face to face relationships and men have shoulder to shoulder relationships, as they talk less and do more.

How would this affect men and women in the workplace? Women who have a falling out with a female colleague feel that they are friends or they are not and will even sabotage a friend's work whom they have grown apart from. Men can have disagreements even to the point of violence and them go to the bar together after 5 p.m. This male behaviour perplexes women who perceive this inconsistency to represent superficiality. Women's behaviour can perplex men who think that women take workplace relationships too seriously.

Why do we have these differences? We can understand the necessity for reproductive difference, but why brain difference? The reason is: **We are cave people!**

Women needed to hear children cry because they were the primary caregivers. They needed to be able to focus on colour and texture to differentiate between berries that were poisonous and nutritious. They needed to be able to multi-task so they could deal with the domicile, the children and the elderly simultaneously. Women needed to develop relationships that held the community together.

Men needed to focus on speed and movement so they could recognize the location and speed of supper. They needed the adrenaline so they could chase down that supper and go into risky and dangerous areas where they too might become supper. Men needed to be single minded so they could protect the family and community and provide for them. Men needed to develop relationships with those they could trust their lives with on the hunt or during warfare.

Does this sound like your workplace? Probably not. We certainly are no longer carrying out gathering expeditions and dangerous hunts to survive. But unfortunately, with the exception of a little less hair, we haven't changed much – biologically speaking – from our ancestors time.

The differences mentioned above that were so essential to survival at one time can create miscommunication and conflict in our society and workplace today. They can fuel stereotypes such as men are not nurturing or women are over emotional. These biological differences hold true across the board for women who are very feminine to women who are tomboys. They hold true for effeminate men to roughhousing guys.

Gay and straight differences

Even for homosexual men and women the biological differences for the different sexes hold true. A woman will make more elaborate and subtle colour distinctions than a man will even if she is a tomboy and he is gay. From a biological perspective in relation to the differences we discuss above, a gay man has more in common with a straight man than with a straight or lesbian woman.

Even in light of the many shows on television highlighting the great clothing sense of gay men, the fact remains that the scientific data does not line up. There are gay slobs out there that can't even pair their socks. They just aren't on television.

But there are some biological differences between heterosexual and homosexual people. Must of this data is recent, yet it shows the possible impact of how our biology controls much of what we think and how we think it.

Sibling studies

Most of the evidence for a genetic influence on human sexual orientation comes from family and twin studies. Homosexuality clusters in particular families, especially among siblings. Thus, the brothers of gay men are reported to have about a 22% chance of themselves being gay, whereas the brothers of heterosexual men have only about a 4% chance of being gay.

Similarly, the sisters of lesbians have an increased chance of being lesbian. This clustering in largely sex-specific: the existence of a lesbian in a family has little effect on the chances that her brothers will be gay, or vice versa.[15]

Cell differences

The third interstitial nucleus of the anterior hypothalamus or INAH is a small group of cells in the region of the hypothalamus known in animal studies to be involved in the generation of male-typical sex behavior.

This group of cells is generally larger in men than women. A 1991 autopsy study found that the cell group was smaller, on average, in gay men than in straight men. A more recent study replicated this finding, although the magnitude of the difference was less. This latter study also reported that there was a difference in cell density. There was a higher density (more cells per cubic millimeter) in the gay men.

The researchers commented that the total number of cells may be the same in gay and straight men, but are formed more closely in the gay men, perhaps because they did not form so many synapses[16] during development.

These findings support the prenatal hormone theory, that the level of testosterone during a critical prenatal/perinatal period of development, affects the ultimate size of the cell group, as well as causing atypical sex behavior in adulthood.[17]

Changes in the cerebral cortex

There is a report that the anterior commissure, a fiber bundle connecting the left and right sides of the cerebral cortex, is larger in women than men, and larger in gay men than in straight men.[18]

Handedness

There seems to be little or no difference in the handedness of heterosexual men and women, but most studies have found that gay men and lesbians are significantly more likely to be non-righthanded (left-handed or mixed-handed) than straight people of the same sex. Hand preference is observable before birth, though it can change as a result of birth trauma and the like. The observation of increased non-righthandness in gay people is therefore consistent with the idea that sexual orientation is influenced by prenatal processes.[19]

What do these findings about men and women and their brain differences mean? This information on diversity gives us understanding to work more effectively across the gender divide, minimizing our stereotypes and inclination to assume we know the reality of someone who is different than us in a gendered way.

ENDNOTES

1. 57.8% of women of working age are in the workforce, 67.8% of men of working age are as well. There are 15,949,700 people in the paid Canadian workforce, of which 13,002,000 are full time and 2,949,500 are part time. Of the 13,002,000 full time workers, 7,558,300 are men and 5,441,900 are women. Of the 2,949,500 part time workers 921,300 are male and 2,028,200 are women. Statistics Canada, 2004. *Labour force, employed and unemployed, numbers and rates, by provinces.*

2. Professor John Corso at Penn State during the 1950s and 1960s demonstrated that females hear better than males. John Corso, "Age and Sex Differences in Thresholds," *Journal of the Acoustical Society of America, 1959.* John Corso, "Aging and Auditory Thresholds in Men and Women," *Archives of Environmental Health,* 1963.

3. "Chapter Four – A History of the Doctrine of Cerebral Localization", *A History of Neurology,* Walter Riese

4. "Sex Differences in Hemispheric Asymmetries of the Human Brain", *Nature,* Herbert Lansdell, 1964.
"Sex Differences in Human Brain Asymmetry: A Critical Survey", *Behavioral and Brain Sciences,* Jeannette McGlone, 1980.
"Sex Differences in Brain Gray and White Matter in Healthy Young Adults: Correlations with Cognitive Performance", *Journal of Neuroscience,* 1999.

5. or broke a bra strap.

6. "The Conundrum of the glass ceiling", *The Economist,* July 23, 2005.

7. "Sex Differences in Human Neonatal Social Perception," Jennifer Connellan, Simon Baron-Cohen and Associates, *Infant Behaviour and Development,* 2000.
"The Dynamics of Primate Retinal Ganglion Cells", Ehud Kaplan and Ethan Bernardete, *Progress in Brain Research,* 2001.
"Sex-Specific Development Changes in Amygdala Responses to Affective Faces," William Killgore, Mika Oki, and Deborah Yurgelun-Todd, *NeuroReport,* 2001.
"Gender Differences in Regional Cerebral Activity During Sadness," Frank Schneider, Ute Habel and Associates, *Human Brain Mapping,* 2000.

8. "The Conundrum of the glass ceiling", *The Economist,* July 23, 2005.

9. *Why Gender Matters,* Leonard Sax, M.D., Ph.D., 2005. 90% of all scholarly work on hormonal responses to stress has been done exclusively on males assuming that males and females were wired the same way. Few studied women.

10. "Why Are Most Drowing Victims Men? Sex Differences in Aquatic Skills and Behaviours," Jonathan Howland and Associates, *American Journal of Public Health,* 1996.

11. *Women Don't Ask: Negotiation and the Gender Divide*, Linda Babcock and Sara Laschever, 2003.

12. *Labour force, employed and unemployed, numbers and rates, by provinces*, Statistics Canada, 2004.

13. "Female Grads Make Less Than Males", *Regina Leader Post*, April 27, 2004.

14. For more information on this submission, see *www.bpw.canada.com*.

15. "Evidence of familial nature of male homosexuality", Pillard, R. C., & Weinrich, J. D. (1986). *Archives of General Psychiatry*.
"Familial aggregation of female sexual orientation", *American Journal of Psychiatry*, Bailey, J. M., & Benishay, D. S. (1993).

16. Synapse: the junction point of two neurons, across which a nerve impulse passes.

17. "Two sexually dimorphic cell groups in the human brain", *Journal of Neuroscience*, Allen, L. S., Hines, M., Shryne, J. E., & Gorski, R. A., 1989.
"The interstitial nuclei of the human anterior hypothalamus: an investigation of variation with sex, sexual orientation, and hiv status". *Hormones and Behavior*, Byne, W., Tobet, S., Mattiace, L. A., Lasco, M. S., Kemether, E., Edgar, M. A., Morgello, S., Buchsbaum, M. S., & Jones, L. B., 2001.
"A difference in hypothalamic structure between heterosexual and homosexual men." LeVay, S.,1991.
"Termination of the hormone-sensitive period for differentiation of the sexually dimorphic nucleus of the preoptic area in male and female rats". Brain Research. Developmental Brain Research, *Science*, Rhees, R. W., Shryne, J. E., & Gorski, R. A., 1990.
"Role of the developing rat testis in differentiation of the neural tissues mediating mating behavior." *Journal of Comparative and Physiological Psychology*, Grady, K. L., Phoenix, C. H., & Young, W. C., 1965.

18. "Sexual orientation and the size of the anterior commissure in the human brain", *Proceedings of the National Academy of Sciences of the United States of America*, Allen, L. S., & Gorski, R. A., 1992.

19. "Handedness in the human fetus", *Neuropsychologia*, Hepper, P. G., Shahidullah, S., & White, R, 1991.
"Sexual orientation and handedness in men and women: a meta-analysis", *Psychological Bulletin*, Lalumiere, M. L., Blanchard, R., & Zucker, K. J., 2000
"Queer science: The use and abuse of research into homosexuality", *MIT Press*, LeVay, S., 1996.
"Handedness, sexual orientation, and gender-related personality traits in men and women", *Archives of Sexual Behavior*, Lippa, R. A., 2003.
"Dermatoglyphics, handedness, sex, and sexual orientation", *Archives of Sexual Behavior*, Mustanski, B. S., Bailey, J. M., & Kaspar, S., 2002.

CHAPTER ELEVEN
Leaping the Generation Gaps

Like a pearl, our individual diversity is many-layered. We are defined not just by our gender, racial background and religious beliefs. We are also defined by our age.

Some would say that we are only as old as we feel, but our age identity is more than the number of areas that ache when the weather changes. Our age identity has been shaped by our experiences in youth and early adulthood. These experiences impact our values and how we interact in the workplace. They affect our beliefs about work, power, and money.

Like other kinds of diversity, differences in age groups in an organization can create conflict. When we work in a team with people primarily from our age group, we may have less conflict because we have experienced many of the same things and seem to speak the same language. We know what is important in the work we do and how we do it.

Different age groups have different perspectives. If we can understand what motivates people from a particular age group, we can function more effectively in a multi-generational workforce.

For leaders, understanding generational groups is extremely important if we wish to recruit and keep the best workforce.

For the first time, there are four distinct groups in the industrialized workforce:[1] Traditionalists (or the mature generation), Baby Boomers, Generation X and Generation Y.

Traditionalists or the Mature Generation

Traditionalists were born between 1922 and 1945[2] and their childhood and early adulthood were defined by conflict and strife. They grew up during the depression, the 'dirty thirties', WWII and the Korean War.

They value steady, profitable employment and trust the organization to guarantee their success. They are loyal to the organization and willing to pay their dues to climb the corporate ladder. They understand the hierarchy in the organization and they respect it. They know that their supervisor can define their opportunities and they demonstrate respect towards that person, regardless of that individual's skill and knowledge.

The Traditionalist's attitudes towards the workplace include loyalty, dedication, sacrifice, compliance, and diligence. Their goal is to contribute to the organization's success and legacy. Today they stay in organizations that are loyal to their employees and in job searches are attracted to organizations that are stable.

They need to be supported in any change efforts as they resist change more than any of the other three groups.

They often have succeeded with less general education than their younger colleagues but have more experience and perhaps more job specific training. To feel valued, they need their experience to be seen as important as other people's newer expertise and education.

With colleagues, they maintain formal relationships. They work hard, focusing on activity and process. They take their cue from their supervisor and those with more experience in the organization regarding appropriate behaviour. In a leadership role, they are more likely to be directive versus collaborative and expect respect automatically with the title of leader.

Most of the 'C' positions and board members are comprised of this generation. They are the 'Canadian Establishment'. [3]

Baby Boomers

The Baby boomers were born between the years 1946 and 1964.

Unlike the previous generation, Boomers lack any childhood recollection of World War II. Although the term "Boomer" is now in global use, the generation is also known in Europe as the Generation of 1968 for protests that led to the fall of the French government. Cheap, easy travel, relative peace, inexpensive and widespread college education, and mass communications created by the generation before made the philosophical and cultural awakening possible for the Boomer generation.

More than Traditionalists, Baby Boomers desire a more democratic, flat organizational structure with higher control over their work. This democratic perspective might be seen reflected in their willingness to slightly bend the rules or challenge authority, and in having relaxed relationships with superiors and friendly relationships with co-workers. They bond with colleagues and their loyalty is to their team or department, versus the company at large.

A Boomer's self worth is tied to what he or she does for a living. Working long hours and traveling long distances are seen as medals of honour in the battle to build a career. Today Boomers are the most likely of the four groups to take work on holiday, have their office cell phone on over the weekend or work after dinner in the evening. Boomers really do live to work (versus Traditionalists who work to live).

The Baby Boomers are the first and last generation to expect job security. Where traditionalists did not take for granted the employment they had, boomers were raised in a time of optimism, economic growth and expansion. They had seen a man land on the moon! Anything was possible!

Once in the workplace, this desire for longevity defined their career strategy. Baby boomers attempted to align themselves with those who could assist their career aspirations. This political bent was reflected in the discretionary distribution of information. Until ten years ago and the growing advent of information sharing via technology, distributing information on a need to know basis created power. (You will see shortly how this strategy creates conflict with Gen X and Gen Y colleagues.)

Baby Boomers are not receptive to change that they do not control, and that is why in part the downsizing in organizations through the 1990s was felt so deeply. For Traditionalists, job security wasn't an expectation, but a nice perk. Downsized Boomers were angry and resentful that their jobs changed or were dissolved. They felt they had a right to their positions – hadn't they worked hard and done all the right things to ensure they were secure?

As organizations began to embrace working in teams, relationships became more important than processes. Boomers generally have more skills in this area than Traditionalists who may need more assistance in being effective coaches and mentors.

As leaders, Baby Boomers are more collaborative than the generation preceding them. This collaborative attitude is facilitated by their more personal relationships in their workplaces with colleagues and subordinates.

As of 2005, the oldest Boomers are approaching retirement age. The younger members of the generation are still in their forties, and many have yet to leave their mark upon history and still have time in which to do so. Some who already have are Bobby Orr, the hockey player (born in 1948), John Belushi, the actor and comedian (1949), Steve Jobs, the founder of Apple Computer and cellist Yo-Yo Ma (1950), Tom Hanks, the actor (1956), Diana, Princess of Wales, Michael J. Fox, and Wayne Gretzky (1961), Jim Carrey (1962), and Mike Meyers (1963).

I imagine there is a difference between how Bobby Orr and Mike Meyers see the world, as they bookend the time frame for baby boomer births. They could both be considered to be born in 'cross over' years – the last few years of one generation or the first few of the next. For example, I was born in 1962 and I see some of my behaviours as boomer behaviours and others reflected in the Generation X description following. These are generational groupings so if you were born within a couple of years of an end or beginning date, ask yourself which generational group you are most like and in what ways. Also remember that these are generational trends and are here to give you ideas of the diversity within the age groups, not to define the group in absolute behaviour.

Generation X

The term Generation X was coined by Jane Deverson who was asked by the magazine *Woman's Own* to conduct a series of interviews with British teenagers in 1964. The study revealed teenagers "sleep together before they are married, don't believe in God, dislike the Queen and don't respect parents". Discussion of the results were deemed to be unsuitable for publication in the magazine.

Deverson, in an attempt to save her research, worked with Hollywood correspondent Charles Hamblett to create a book about the study titled *Generation X*.

The term Generation X was later popularized in 1991 when Douglas Coupland's popular novel *Generation X: Tales for an Accelerated Culture* was published. The main character, Kevin, is a Canadian trailing edge Baby Boomer who denies affiliation with his older sister and friends, all Boomers. Kevin and his cohorts are all over-educated, under-employed, pay sky-rocketing living expenses and are occasionally forced to move back home with their parents. "X is a category of people who wanted to hop off the merry-go-round of status, money, and social climbing that so often frames modern existence," said Copeland.

It was after the publication of Coupland's book that the term began being used as a name for the generation by the media and later by the general public. The media introduced Generation X as a group born between 1965 and 1980 who were flannel-wearing, alienated, overeducated, underachieving slackers with body piercing, who drank franchise-store coffee and had to work at McJobs, concepts that had some truth to them but were mostly stereotypes.

This generation is sometimes also known as the Baby Busters, or Busters. In continental Europe, the generation is often known as Generation E, or simply known as the Nineties Generation. In France, the term *Génération Bof* is in use, with "bof" being a French word for "whatever", considered by some French people

113

to be the defining Gen-X saying. In Iran, they are called the Burnt Generation. In some Latin American countries the name "Crisis Generation" is sometimes used due to the recurring financial crisis in the region during those years.

In Western countries, Generation X consists of far fewer people than the baby boom generation and has had correspondingly less impact on popular culture.

Generation X has survived a hurried childhood of divorce, latchkeys, space shuttle explosions, open classrooms, widespread political corruption, inflation and recession, national malaise, and environmental disaster.

Divorce became common place and affected families of all social and economic backgrounds. Naturally, Gen Xers were affected by the continual bombardment of images of the nuclear family and feelings of inadequacy and isolation from society resulted. As young adults, maneuvering through a sexual barricade of AIDS and blighted courtship rituals, they date cautiously.

The expansion of the Internet rendered face-to-face communication secondary, books beside the point, near-infinite knowledge on hand at all times, and tech-related jobs a hot commodity. In jobs, Gen Xers embrace risk and prefer free agency to corporate life. Sometimes criticized as "slackers", they nevertheless were widely credited with a new growth of entrepreneurship and the resulting dot-com boom.

Generation X grew up in the shadow of the boomers. Their parents were likely to be dual-income and created children who had to take care of themselves. This leads to children of this generation being independent, self-reliant and pragmatic.

They saw their parents downsized, outsized and right-sized and became disillusioned with the corporate world. They saw their parents live to work and chose to work to live instead. Their work is only a part of who they are and their self-esteem is not primarily defined by their career. In this, they are different from the Boomer generation.

Gen Xers are unimpressed by authority or seniority, and think that skills are more important than titles. This is because skills make your career mobile when you are shown the door and relationships do not.

Gen Xers grew up with personal computers in every home, the fall of the Berlin wall, and the fear of Canada's downfall with Quebec referendums. Their latchkey life as youth led them to be techno-literate and good at working alone and on their own. In the workplace, they want to maintain this independence that they are familiar with.

Gen Xers are loyal to their manager as opposed to their department or organization. This means that if their supervisor moves to a different company they might go as well if the opportunity presents itself, especially if their relationship with their supervisor is informal and collegial. They engage in open dialogue if conflict erupts and have little patience with the 'games' they see boomers play around conflict and politics.

They are more likely to bail if they perceive rankism$_4$ where a boomer or traditionalist, especially one who has only a few years to pension, would ride out the humiliating behaviour of their superior. Unlike Traditionalists for whom job change is a stigma and for Boomers who see as a career stall, job change for a Gen Xer is seen as necessary to build a mobile career.

Gen Xers are not prepared to work hard if they do not feel considerable loyalty towards them by the organization. They want to know what the organization can do for them. This cynicism is due to the lack of loyalty they saw organizations show previous generations.

Gen Xers have little patience with the process, politics and activity of boomers. They focus on results. They wonder, "Why isn't the organization striving to get results; why is efficiency more important than effectiveness?"

In leadership roles, Gen Xers are likely to be fair, straightforward, flexible, brutally honest and non-political. They are open to changing the rules if required, work with little supervision, and demonstrate an informal, multi-tasking work style.

115

Generation Y

The Y in *Generation Y* comes from the name Generation X given to the previous generation5. This generation born between 1981 and 2001 has also been called the Millennial generation or the Echo Generation.

Demographic numbers in North America mark the echo as slightly smaller than the Baby Boom, but much larger than Generation X.

A good way to define the boundaries of this generation are by the attacks on 9/11 in New York in 2001. People who were not yet born in 2001 or were too young to remember or understand what happened on that day would be grouped into Generation Z, while people who were of age, out of school, and into adult life would be grouped into Generation X. The 9/11 attacks epitomizes Gen Y. It caps off the insecurity created by Y2K and school shootings. This generation was taught that life could be short so don't waste it.

In many wealthy countries, the 1980s and 1990s were a period of rapidly falling birthrates. In Southern Europe and Japan, Generation Y is dramatically smaller than any of its predecessors, and their childhood was marked by small families, small classes at school and school closures. In the Soviet Union during the 1980s, there was a "baby boom echo" similar to that in Canada and the United States, and Generation Y there is relatively large; however, birth rates in the 1990s fell to extremely low levels.

In Eastern Europe, Generation Y is the first generation without mature memories of Communism or dictatorship. In newly rich countries such as South Korea or Greece, Generation Y has known nothing but developed world standards of living, while their grandparents often grew up in developing world conditions, causing considerable social changes and inter-generational difficulties as the young reject many traditional ways of life.

This generation is the most globally aware. They are generally very tolerant towards multiculturalism and it is not uncommon for post-1970s born children to grow up dating people outside their own racial or ethnic group, as well as having a wide range in friends.

Generation Y is the first generation to grow up with the Internet

116

in a developed, prolific form, including music downloads, instant messaging and cell phones. This digital world view versus the analog world view that the first three generations embrace (especially boomers and traditionalists) makes Gen Ys perceive the workplace very differently.

In an analog world, we function in process. Consider a movie on VHS. You watch it from beginning to end. In a digital world, a DVD allows you to skip over what you don't want to see, review the interesting parts and watch the segments in any order you wish. Certainly, with enough time, you could painstakingly rewind and replay a VHS tape, but few Gen Ys would have the patience for it. Time is something that this generation is not willing to waste. The axiom "patience is a virtue" has been lost on this generation. Patience is a virtue to boomers and traditionalists and no one else.

Gen Y has also come to mean Gen "Why?". Unless you can explain the rationale for doing something, they will resist taking action. In generations before, where authority held sway, employees would do what was required, often without seeing the reason for doing so. But this Game Boy™ generation wants to see results, and tie their efforts to consequence. "Because we do it that way", "there must be a reason I just don't know what it is", "you don't need to know"– are all responses that might have worked with Boomers and even Gen Xers but will get you nowhere with a Generation Y co-worker or subordinate.

Generation Y has no respect for authority based on title or seniority. There are several reasons for this.

The first is family size. In a large family like I was born into (five girls, one boy) our opinions were often listened to but rarely sought or followed. With a household of that size, following individual preferences would have created chaos. Someone had to be in charge, and it wasn't us! It was our parents. However, in a family system with only one or two children, children are often invited into the adult world. Particularly in single parent families, they are treated as partners, not offspring. This helped Gen Ys see themselves equal in decision-making authority to those a generation older. This is also why they expect equitable relationships with superiors in the workplace.

117

The second reason is that Gen Ys may see those in authority as incompetent. In their digital world they respect demonstrated competence and advanced skills. This is the generation that programmed their parents' VCRs and taught them how to make folders in their email. They highly value technical expertise as they see it as the conduit for problem solving and achievement.

Traditionalists and Boomers often do what they are requested to do because the one asking is their boss. Gen Ys are more likely to do what they agree with, what makes sense. If it doesn't, they are more than willing to challenge their supervisor regarding the logic behind the request. They have less fear of losing their job or being penalized in some way. They place a strong value on enjoying their work and having their opinion counted, so losing their job is a lesser evil than staying where they are not valued. They want to find work and create a life that has meaning. They are willing to continue looking for that opportunity until they find it.

Gen Ys can be loyal. However, they don't automatically have loyalty to their organization, department or manager, like the previous generations. They are loyal to those they see walking the talk. They value integrity and commit to those who display it. They do not have loyalty to those who tell them to do one thing, and then themselves do the other. They have no tolerance for advice, only example. They are willing to follow those who they find compelling and could change jobs at a moment's notice to be on a team that they find more meaningful. This quick willingness to move may be seen by previous generations as demonstrating a lack of consistency, dependability and loyalty.

This group is the most confident and expectant of the four. They ask not what they can do for a prospective employer, but what a prospective employer can do for them. "What is the signing bonus? How quickly will I receive a raise? Who will I get to work with and learn from?" They are fearless and open to debating and challenging the ideas of others to achieve compromise or collaboration. Where Boomers are more cautious in their work-place relationships, Gen Ys may be seen to be aggressive and unreflective. They desire change, not only when necessary but as a guarantee of variety in their work. They don't think outside the box, they live outside the box.

Our Future

"When 76 industry associations were surveyed, 62 out of 76 indicated skills shortages exist, 73 out of 76 said they expected shortages over the next 5 years – especially in health care, trades, rural and remote areas."

Canada West Foundation Survey, 2004 [6]

As organizations, we need new workers. Certainly we need to attract employees from non-traditional sources such as immigration. But we also need to encourage workers currently in the workplace to stay longer and for younger workers to commit to our organizations.

As individuals, if we interact with others based on how we see the world, we will not be as successful as if we seek to understand them and work with that understanding. Generations are a perfect example of this. The term generation gap describes how differently we think from another generation. Historically it has been that the older generation has attempted to impose their values and ways on the generation following and the generation following has been resentful and rebellious. This is perfectly understandable – don't we resent those who invalidate who we are and try to make us into them?

As the four generations mix in the workplace and there is as great a chance of a Gen Xer trying to impose her or his way of work on a Boomer as the other way around, we need to take age diversity seriously.

We can leap the generational gaps that exists between these four groups if we understand what motivates each one and how they are unique in their diversity.

ENDNOTES

1. In non-industrial workforces such as agriculture, families would work together and many generations would have been represented.

2. There is disagreement between demographers regarding the start and end dates of each generation. The numbers identified as birth start and end dates may be different by a year or two from information you have received from other sources.

3. C meaning any job with Chief at the beginning such as Chief Executive Officer, Chief Administrative Officer, Chief Operating Officer.

4. Rankism is when differences in rank are used as an excuse to abuse, humilate, exploit or subjugate. For more on this, see the book *Somebodies and Nobodies*, Robert W. Fuller (2003).

5. Y immediately following X in the alphabet.

6. "West faces skills shortage , trade associations indicate", *Globe and Mail*, June 2, 2004.

CHAPTER TWELVE
Perspectives on Time

A colourful, well worn public bus rumbles down a dusty deserted road on a Caribbean isle. The bus stops at the bus stop to take on the lone woman standing there impatiently.

"You are late!" says the woman.

"I am not late!" says the bus driver.

"You are 43 seconds late!" replies the passenger, pointing at her watch.

A head pops down from a man riding atop of the bus, *"You are now a whole minute late! I will be late for my appointment!"*

Behind the bus, a traveler on a bicycle is brought up short by the stopped bus, *"Oh no, 'mon',"* he cries, *"Total grid lock!"*

(Television commercial for Malibu Rum)

Every time I see this commercial I chuckle, as no doubt many other Canadians who see the commercial do as well. Why? What is amusing? If the scenario was in Toronto or Vancouver or even Moose Jaw, the conversation would not have been amusing; it would have been real life. People in a hurry, people running late, people not respecting each other's time.

Up until 200 years ago, most non-aboriginal Canadians and Americans were living much as their ancestors had lived when they first came to North America. They fished and farmed. The people were closely bound to the dynamics of agricultural rhythms, tides, weather and seasons. In Canada, not many people had clocks but everyone was acutely aware of time's passage, especially in nature. In this intensely agricultural society, rural life was unending hard work and operated under deadlines imposed by approaching darkness, unfavourable weather or the growing season. "Making hay while the sun shines" was taken literally.[1]

In Europe, massive urbanization had started and many Europeans moved from rural locations to cities to work in industry. Economic pressures of industrialization required them to become aware of time as a value.

As Canadians began to urbanize, the pressure of the clock came to visit them as well. Agricultural environmental pressure eventually gave way to smaller increments of clock time as the clock became the tool of industrial taskmasters.

Western Europeans and North Americans adopted timeliness as a virtue. The protestant work ethic dominant in the new world lived parallel with the clock watching paradigm. Being 'on time', not 'wasting time', using every minute available for productivity became virtuous.

> *"Remember that time is money."*
> *Benjamin Franklin*[2]

> *"A woman is under obligation to so arrange the hours and pursuits of her family as to promote systematic and habitual industry; and if, by late breakfasts, irregular hours of meals, and other hindrances of this kind, she interferes with or refrains from promoting regular industry in others, she is accountable to God for all the waste of time consequent in her negligence."*
> *Catherine Beecher, A Treatise On Domestic Economy, 1841*[3]

Every culture has different ways of organizing time. Some cultures are rigidly bound by their schedules and deadlines while other cultures have a relaxed attitude about detailed plans and promptness. Polychronic time stresses involvement with people and completion of transactions rather than an adherence to a

122

preset schedule. North Americans generally have a monochronic time orientation and for most, time is money, to be used, saved and spent. North Americans set schedules and appointments and tend to prioritize events and move through the process 'controlling' the time allotted each part of the process. 4

In Mexico, there is a relaxed polychronic attitude towards time. Although time is a concern, Mexicans do not allow schedules to interfere with experiences involving their family or friends. The culture is more people-oriented than task-oriented. It is important to be on time for very important appointments, but one should always expect to wait, as a meeting may not end simply because the next scheduled appointment has arrived.

Most First Nations follow a polychronic time view. A friend of mine was working as an economic development consultant with several Indian bands and was constantly frustrated with the poly-chronic time perspective on the reserve. He wanted to schedule a specific time to meet with the client, have the meeting and leave. He often found the meetings did not start on time, but his clients wanted him to stay until they were satisfied with the discussion.

Today we recognize the difference in how time is perceived, yet we usually see monochronic time as good or best and polychronic time as bad. We use words such as 'siesta' time, 'Indian' time, 'island' time, and 'Caribbean' time to describe those on polychronic time.

Cultural influences also affect our perspective on time. In Canada, 'Indian' time continued to exist as aboriginal communities were often shut off from working in mainstream industrialized society (sometimes through the pass and permit system and sometimes for other reasons). Aboriginal populations were also more concentrated in rural and northern areas where fishing and hunting were the way of life. They were less influenced by the European time paradigm and continued to view time as was appropriate and not as defined by industrialization.

The ongoing debate in Saskatchewan about Daylight Savings Time illustrates the difference between industrialized and agricultural lifestyles. If you are in agriculture, daylight savings time is almost irrelevant. You work when the sun is up, you get out of the field when the sun goes down. You work through the night when the crop must come off, when cows are calving or when you have a sick horse. That is oversimplifying their work issues, but you see the point. The appropriate time to do something is more important than being on schedule.

In Canada, we have more and more people in the workplace coming from areas in the world where 'Caribbean' or 'siesta' time is the agreement for time. We have more people entering the workplace coming from an 'Indian' time perspective. In fact, 75% of the world perceives time in a polychronic way. However, most Canadian workplaces function in the monochronic time mindset and Canadians generally have little patience with those on Caribbean time, siesta time, island time and Indian time.

We not only have agreements in society about time in the polychronic and monochronic sense described above, we also have agreements about when is best to start and end our day.

"Early to bed and early to rise will
make a man healthy, wealthy and wise."
Benjamin Franklin

"The early bird catches the worm."
Anonymous

Quotes like these infer that if you are a night owl instead of an early bird, you will be unhealthy, poor, stupid, undisciplined and lazy. We place more value in our society on being early to bed and early to rise than late to bed and late to rise. We value the early bird behaviour over a night owl's late to bed inclination.

Carolyn Schur, author of *Birds of a Different Feather - Early Birds and Night Owls Talk About Their Characteristic Behaviours*[5] believes that up to 25% of the population may be night owls, with a slightly smaller percentage early birds and 60% being Intermediates. (Intermediates favour a bedtime between 11 p.m. and midnight and awake time between 7 and 8 a.m.)

Many people think that time preference is something a person could change if they wanted to. But trying to become an early bird when you are a night owl is like writing with your right hand when you are left handed. Certainly you can force yourself to do it, but you will be less productive and it will feel uncomfortable and unnatural.

This is because internally we are controlled by a master clock which controls sleep and wakefulness, body temperature and metabolic rate. One of the most important factors in whether we are early birds or night owls is our body temperature. When our normal daily body temperature is at its lowest, we are the most inclined towards sleep. When our normal daily body temperature is at its highest, we are the most alert. Exactly when these changes happen determines whether we will be an early bird (who loves to leap out of bed at 6 a.m. with vim and vigor) or a night owl (who loves stay to in bed until noon and then work into the wee hours).

It's not fun being a night owl in an early bird world. We see our society's opinion of night owls and early birds in the language we use every day. The night is called the 'dark' hours, staying in bed until noon is called 'sleeping in'; early birds get up 'bright and early' and are 'set for the day'.

Night owls are often reprimanded in the workplace due to lateness in the morning. They are often teased by colleagues regarding their schedules. There is pressure placed on them to be cheerful first thing when they still feel tired. This value ridden perspective of time creates low self-esteem and inhibits night owl's career success.

In Carolyn Schur's book, Night Owls are quoted as saying:

"I hear the kibitzing in the office. It's not so much even things that are said, but the looks, the glance - very cutting." (Darcy) [6]

"Sometimes my friends will bug me. They'll say "Well, what time did you get up today, ten, eleven?" There will be shots taken at you." (John) [7]

Ironically, it may be the night owls we need the most in the 21st century workplace. According to Statistics Canada, up to 30% of workers in Canada are involved in non-traditional schedules. Non traditional work schedules are defined as working other than 9-5, Monday to Friday, 35 to 40 hours a week. It can include

125

extended hours, rotating shifts and permanent night or evening shifts.8

In a world that demands a 24 hour lifestyle, it is the early birds who have the problems in adjusting to shift work and staying alert at night. As the workplace changes and the demand for longer days, extended days, shift work and working at night increases, early birds will find it more difficult to cope.

"The profound irony is that as much as society denigrates night owls, it is the early birds who are fast becoming albatrosses as they are less able to meet the challenges of the schedules of the new workplace".

Carlyn Schur, author and lecturer on shift work and fatigue.9

We have different ways of organizing time culturally. Individually, we have different biological time. Whether culturally or biologically, these differences can create true conflict in the workplace. By knowing who we are, and not jumping to negative stereotypes of others, we can work towards a more effective workplace.

ENDNOTES

1. *On Time - How America Has Learned to Live by the Clock*, Carlene E. Stephens, 2002.

2. *Advice to A Young Tradesman*, Written by an Old One, Benjamin Franklin, 1748.

3. Quoted in *Keeping Watch: A History of American Time*, Michael O'Malley, 1990.

4. *Managing Cultural Differences*, Philip R. Harris, Robert T. Moran and Sarah V. Moran, 2004.

5. *Birds of a Different Feather - Early Birds and Night Owls Talk About Their Characteristic Behaviours*, Carolyn Schur, 1994.

6. *Birds of a Different Feather - Early Birds and Night Owls Talk About Their Characteristic Behaviours*, Carolyn Schur, 1994.

7. *Birds of a Different Feather - Early Birds and Night Owls Talk About Their Characteristic Behaviours*, Carolyn Schur, 1994.

8. Carolyn Schur in interview 2005.

9. Carolyn Schur in interview 2005.

CHAPTER THIRTEEN
The Other Brain

If you have ever been through a Meyer Briggs, True Colours or DISC survey, you may have been told you have a brain, but only half of it is working. The two different sides of our brain control two different modes of thinking. Each of us prefers one mode over the other. Both sides of the brain can reason but by different strategies, and one side may be dominant.

Experimentation has shown that the two different sides or hemispheres of the brain are responsible for different ways of thinking. The left is considered analytical in approach while the right is described as holistic or global. Left brainers prefer to learn in a step-by-step or linear sequential format beginning with details leading to a conceptual understanding of a skill. Right brainers prefer a simultaneous or lateral approach to learning, beginning with a general concept and then going on to specifics.

Left brainers respond to word meaning, logical plans, can recall people's names, are punctual, logical, sequential, rational, and objective. Right brainers are random, intuitive, holistic, synthesizing, subjective, impulsive, and can recall people's faces.

In discussing this chapter with a colleague, we compared our very different ways of thinking. She is more left brained and I am more right brained. She is one of the editors of this book and has compared my writing style to throwing a bunch of stuff on a table and hoping it will fit together. She believes that a framework is necessary for pieces to fall logically into place beneath or within the framework. I told her that I don't think that the word 'framework' is in my vocabulary and logic is overrated.

Left brain and right brain differences tie in to what we find is important in a task or project. Left brainers are more likely to see what needs to be done and how it needs to be done. Right brainers are more likely to see how what needs to be done ties to the global whole and who should be involved. Left brainers ask what and how, right brainers ask why and whom.

Let's consider the four major differences between left and right brain dominance:

Linear or Holistic Processing

The left side of the brain processes information in a linear manner. It processes from part to whole. It takes pieces, lines them up, and arranges them in a logical order; then it draws conclusions.

The right brain however, processes from whole to parts, holistically. It starts with the answer. It sees the big picture first, not the details. A left brainer outlines the book and then writes it, a right brainer writes the book and then outlines it.

Sequential or Random Processing

Left brainers process in sequence. They are list makers and enjoy making master schedules and daily plans. They complete tasks in order and take pleasure in checking them off when they are accomplished. Likewise, learning things in sequence is relatively easy, such as spelling and math.

The right brain, however, is random. A right brainer moves from task to task and back again, and is often seen as being unorganized by their fellow co-workers. I can identify with this characteristic as I was writing 15 chapters of this book, all at one time. A right brainer might get as much done, but perhaps right under the wire. Right brainers are not in love with schedules and lists, except in the most flexible way.

Symbolic or Concrete Processing

The left brain easily processes symbols such as letters, words, and mathematical notations. The left brainer tends to be comfortable with linguistic and mathematical endeavors and can memorize text or mathematical formulas.

The right brain, on the other hand, wants things to be concrete. Right brainers wants to see, feel, or touch the real object. They prefer to see words in context, to see an example of how the formula works, to see a graph or chart of the material being represented.

Logical or Intuitive Processing

The left brain processes in a linear, sequential, logical manner. Left brainers use information piece by piece to solve a problem. They read and listen, looking for the pieces so that they can draw logical conclusions.

When you process primarily on the right side of the brain, you use intuition. Right brainers know the right answer to a technical problem but may not be sure how they got the answer. They may have to start with the answer and work backwards. Right brainers have a gut feeling as to which answer is correct, and are often right.

In writing, it is the left brain that pays attention to mechanics such as spelling, agreement, and punctuation. But the right side pays attention to coherence and meaning; that is, your right brain tells you it "feels" right.

> *"Books on Organizing are written by Left Brainers,*
> *bought by Right Brainers, and never opened."*
>
> *Jeanne Martinson, Right Brainer*

We often recognize that we are not whole. Right brainers and left brainers in business who are successful recognize their brain deficiency. And buy books and go to seminars to rectify the situation.

In his book, *The E-Myth*, Michael E. Gerber describes why business owners fail. He suggests that there are three competencies we need to be successful in business: financial, marketing and technical. For example, if I owned a restaurant, the technical skills involved would be cooking, serving and clearing. The marketing skills would be getting people into the restaurant and having them come back. This would involve designing marketing plans and initiatives. The third element is the financial skill. This is the GST, payroll, bank deposits, and year end.

My experiences as President of Women Entrepreneurs of Saskatchewan highlights this. I spoke to many entrepreneurs about their businesses and their careers. They had one of two complaints. They loved the technical and marketing elements of the business, but hated the bookwork. Or they loved the technical and bookwork, but had no head for the marketing. Successful entrepreneurs know they have to seek out the diversity in others to compliment their skills if they are going to be successful.

In effective teams, people know that both brains have to be in the room. Last year, I was a co-covenor of a national convention. My partner was a left brainer. She saw budget issues that were not even on my radar. I saw potential in the creative things we could do to make the convention world class. We were essential to each other's success. But that didn't mean that we didn't occasionally rub each other the wrong way with our other-brainness.

It is true that books on organizing are written by left brained people (right brained people wouldn't have a clue what to say). They have the theory and the wisdom and assume others just have to learn and follow the process. Unfortunately, the very ideas that left brainers embrace when it comes to time management are the same ideas that right brainers find limit their productivity. For example, left brainers like to make lists, handle pieces of paper only once, file things out of sight and handle details. Right brainers want to have all their 'stuff' out where they can see it and file in piles. Although to a left brainer, this seems like chaos, for the right brainer it is the only way to function effectively.

In this book, we have discussed how it is essential to find out what the small 'd' differences are between ourselves and others we work with. One of the small 'd' differences is whether we are

132

primarily right or left brain dominant. Like early birds and night owls, this difference between people is hard wired.

We need to embrace the 'other brain-ness' that our co-workers bring to our work so that we can have effective, productive teams.

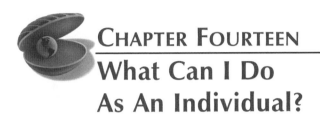

Chapter Fourteen

What Can I Do
As An Individual?

Human beings function in the workplace in an unconscious state. Certainly we are awake, but rarely aware. We function out of habitual reaction, an unconscious state, instead of thoughtful response. Someone says A, we respond with B. Behaviours of others trigger positive and negative responses in us. Our behaviour triggers negative or positive responses in others. We often blame others for the responses they have and for the responses they trigger within us, without looking under the layers to see how our differences create the conflict.

Most people want to have friendly relationships with their colleagues, but sometimes differences make this difficult. The following three ideas are offered in the hope that you can have more collegial and productive relationships with those over the cubicle wall.

Idea #1 – Be Aware when you are reacting instead of responding

In the workplace, people say and do things that create reactions in us. These reactions are instantaneous and habitual. We don't often step back before we react, asking ourselves "I wonder what he meant by that?" or "I wonder why she reacted like that?" We judge people based on their behaviour not based on their intention, yet we judge ourselves on our intentions, not on our behaviour.

Sometimes someone can say something that seems to focus on our 'otherness' and triggers a strong response in us. It may not be an intentional slur, but we perceive it to be so. Examples of triggers may include: being called a 'girl' for some women, 'you people' for most everyone, 'sleepyhead' for a night owl, or 'living in sin' for someone living in a common-law relationship.

We trigger others and we are triggered. One thing we can do to bridge the diversity between ourselves and others is to be courageous. We need to ask for clarification and to offer knowledge about who we are to the other person. We must also be willing to admit our misperceptions when we are offered information about them.

When you are triggered, take a breath and respond instead of react. Ask for clarification in a caring, non-judgmental way. For the sleepyhead comment above, a response could sound like: "When you said 'hey sleepyhead, nice to finally see you at work', I interpreted that to mean that you think I am not carrying my load around here. That wasn't your intention, was it?" This kind of response to your trigger often starts a dialogue that leads to an exploration of not just behaviours but intentions and a more understanding work environment is often the result.

Idea #2 Overcome your natural conflict style

Diversity often creates conflict. When we think one choice is important and someone thinks another choice is equally important, we end up in conflict. Sometimes the two sides do not understand why the other is so adamant about their choice because they haven't sat down to explain their different perspectives.

Consider Jane and John. Jane wants to have their team meetings at 8 a.m. and John wants to have them at 4:00 p.m. She wants to have them in the boardroom at the office and John wants a more casual environment at the coffee shop where everyone goes for breaks. Jane told him he is being pigheaded and he replied in same.

What if Jane told John that when the meetings run more than half an hour (as they often do), she feels she has to choose between picking up her kids from daycare and remaining for the rest of the meeting? What if Jane told John that she is partially deaf and the coffee shop noise makes it difficult to hear clearly, requiring her to miss important comments and to ask the other members of the committee for their notes to cross reference with what she thought she heard?

What if John told Jane that as a single dad, he has to get his son who has special needs to his daycare which doesn't open until 8:30, and an early meeting means he has to make special arrangements which make him nervous as this may upset his son?

This conflict could play out in several ways:

- If John is the manager, he may say "This is the way it is going to be. Deal with it." Jane can keep quiet and show up, and do her best to make arrangements for her children. That is giving in to the *competitive* nature of John's decision.

- Jane could *compromise* and leave the meeting early and be at the daycare slightly late.

- Jane could *avoid* the conflict and not show up at all, which hurts her credibility on the team but deals with her time conflict.

- Jane could *accommodate* John's wishes publicly but then 'forget' to reserve the big table at the coffee shop so they have to go elsewhere.

All of the above choices feed John and Jane's growing discord. It would be much more effective if they discussed their differences so they could find a collaborative perspective, finding a solution that worked for both of them.

Idea #3 Reconsider your joking and teasing

"What the hell would I want to go to a place like Mombassa. I just see myself in a pot of boiling water with all these natives dancing around me."

Toronto Mayor Mel Lastman, referring to his unwillingness to go to where the Association of National Olympic Committees of Africa was meeting because he and his wife, Marilyn, feared snakes.[1]

In the written apology, Lastman characterized the comments as 'off the cuff' and a 'joke'. Poor Mel. Thought he was being funny but was not funny at all.

So why do we get in trouble with humour? We bond with other humans through shared laughter and humour drives that laughter. We use humour to be part of the group and to belong.

But humour and its lightweight cousin, teasing, have to be put in context to what group the joking is about and whether it plays into stereotypes. For example, teasing a man with a Middle Eastern, Asian or southern European background about living with his parents is not respecting the cultural group he is from. 85% of young men of a Greek background, compared to 51% of young men from a British background live with their parents even after post-secondary education and gaining full time employment.[2] 'Teasing' men and women from these cultures about being 'losers' or 'tied to their mother's apron strings' can build conflict even when the person doing the teasing thinks it is okay become it is a 'joke'.

For the last two years I have produced a comedy festival. When I first met with the talent bureau for the comedians, the owner listened intently to the idea. We wanted a multi-day event with clean corporate comics that would appeal to a large group of attendees. It was a fundraiser, so our budget was lean. He told me we hadn't budgeted for funny AND clean. Bar comics who use four letter words, racist and sexist lines were the most economical comics. As comics began to write their own material, focusing on the funny in their own lives, they became more expensive. "The jokes at someone else's expense are always the easiest and cheapest."

I learned many things through those two years as a volunteer producer but that one comment stuck with me. We can be funny and do it without hurting others. It just takes more creativity and more awareness.

ENDNOTES

1. "Toronto Mayor Still Apologizing", *Regina Leader Post*, June 22, 2001. Toronto Mayor Mel Lastman was quoted in the *Toronto Star*. He also said that he didn't want to go where the Association of National Olympic Committees of Africa were meeting because he and his wife, Marilyn, feared snakes and then followed it up with this comment.

2. "A Dutiful Son or a Loser?" *Regina Leader Post*, August 27, 2001. Based on 1991 Statistics Canada data.

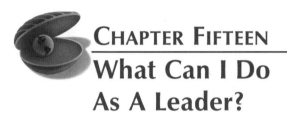

CHAPTER FIFTEEN
What Can I Do
As A Leader?

Not too many years ago, conformity was the workplace standard. Assimilation to the prevailing corporate culture was the norm. Employees learned to fit in, to dress according to company policy, to think only so much as was required to obey the chain of command, and above all, not to rock the boat. Today, we know that the workforce is becoming a diverse, multi-cultural, ever-changing mosaic of individuals.

What does diversity mean to your organization and why should you care? What will workforce diversity mean to each of us, individually? And as leaders? Why do organizations like yours invest time and money into diversity training for employees? And why is it that talking about workforce diversity in our organization can sometimes make us uncomfortable?

Our concept of diversity must evolve to encompass all of the talents, preferences, affiliations, intellects and experiences that make each one of us unique as individuals. Workforce diversity in the 21st century will focus less on what group a person can be identified with, and more on the unique diversity of each individual as the organization's most valuable resource, its human capital.

As leaders, your job is to help maintain a skilled workforce for your organization. From a diversity perspective, the following ideas may help you in that goal:

Idea #1 Know who your staff really are and value their uniqueness

In a diversity leadership workshop I conduct, each participant is given a square piece of cardboard and access to coloured modeling clay. Their task is to complete a figure that symbolizes their uniqueness in the world, including all their knowledge, ways or working and thinking, skills and languages. After the managers' works of art are completed, I line them up in a row, smash them down and cut them into the identical shape with a person-shaped cookie cutter. There are usually gasps as legs and arms are cut off and their individuality is lost in the desire for conformity.

Members of your team have extrinsic value in that you achieve your goals through their efforts. But there is also intrinsic value in people. Our diversity in all its quirks and oddities are the many layers of the pearl that makes us unique. All individuals want to be recognized for their individual gifts.

Idea #2 Know your policies that relate to diversity

- Have you the knowledge to explain to someone in your team how employment equity works and how employees are selected from the four equity groups?

- Do you know your responsibilities under provincial and federal labour law, including occupational health and safety acts?

- Does your workplace have bullying, harassment or respectful workplace policies? Have you taken training in regards to your responsibilities?

- Do you know the difference between stereotyping, tokenism, prejudice, discrimination and systemic discrimination?

- Do you know how to recognize the effects of harassment on a victim? Do you know what you should do if harassment is brought to your attention?

142

- Are you comfortable discussing the possible negative team effects of workplace romance with the people involved? Are you aware of how your workplace harassment policy deals with this issue?

If you answer more no's than yes's to the questions above, you are not alone. But it is in your personal best interest as well as your corporation's to have answers to these questions.

Idea #3 Stay alert for red flags

Many leaders lose valuable staff or have a dysfunctional work team and can't figure out why. They feel like they were blind-sided and often say so. However, leaders that keep their eyes open for red flags might avert trouble before it grabs hold.

Consider these situations:

I. A woman who reports to you leads a team of men and women of various ages and cultural backgrounds. One of the men has refused to give her information she requires. She has told you about the problem and you have spoken to him. He has an issue reporting a woman, especially to a younger woman, but will continue to report to her if forced. But this competitive stance may create passive aggressive behaviour where on the surface he supports or agrees with her, but behind the scenes makes efforts to discredit or undermine her position of power over him.

II. You have two main language groups in the workplace, English-only and French and English speaking. The bi-lingual group gravitates together at meetings, breaks and in social events where they often speak only French. Although some people recognize that most people are more comfortable in their first language, those outside of the language feel excluded. Some members of the English-only speaking group feel resentful. This conflict has escalated and now two separate groups exist. The individual members will not work effectively together with members from the other team.

III. Jokes with sexual innuendos are part of your team's culture. Several new techs from middle eastern backgrounds find the banter unsettling and unprofessional. They have not said anything but are secretly looking for new employment. When an employee does not engage in the informal team conversations, a leader should see this as a red flag. It would be essential to notice the employee's self-isolation before the valued tech takes himself and his skill set elsewhere.

Idea #4 Be aware that different rules apply to you

Employees in your team recognize that you hold the reins to their economic future. You can determine whether they get a promotion, demotion, or are shown the door. Due to this power differential, you must be particularly aware that requests that fall outside the parameters of a staff member's job description may be dangerous. One of the most important situations to consider involves sexual requests or romantic relationships. Consider the following case:

Dennis Carey, a Vice Chairman with the firm Spencer Stuart (a U.S. leader in executive search) began an affair with Marie-Caroline von Weichs who worked out of Spencer Stuart's Frankfurt office. In 2000, he convinced her to move to the States and take over a new company that he and Spencer Stuart were involved in called G100 (a networking club for CEO's). Over the next few years, the couple began another organization called the CEO Academy as well as co-authored a book together, entitled "How to Run a Company".

After finding out he had been less than truthful about when he had separated from and divorced his wife, Marie-Caroline asked him to move out of her Aspen home. Immediately their work relationship changed. He excluded her from meetings, undermined her to G100 members and took days to return her urgent phone calls. On January 8th, 2004, she received a letter from the CFO saying the firm had re-assessed its commitment to G100 and decided not to extend or renew her four year contract when it expired in September 2004. She had been repeatedly told by the Chair of Spencer Stuart that she was doing an excellent job and G100 would pick up her salary directly (instead of through Spencer Stuart).

The opportunity for office romance has increased alongside of our awareness of its dangers. Women and men are working together more intimately than ever before. Historically, many job categories were primarily held by men or primarily held by women and so their everyday work colleagues were often of the same gender. As positions become less gender-specific, more men and women began to work side by side, cubicle by cubicle. This increase in familiarity is wonderful for developing closer working relationships and increasing productivity, however, this same familiarity can lead to workplace conflict, career havoc and lowering of team effectiveness and morale.

Romance will always occur in the workplace. This is where we work long hours with people who truly understand what we do. Those we work with are often more enthusiastic about hearing about our work than anyone else we are close to (including our spouse). Sometimes we emotionally connect engrossing, stimulating work with the people on our team. As well, if we are younger workers, we often meet our first mates in the workplace. Where else do we spend 40 plus hours a week, looking our best and attempting to be respectful, intelligent and useful? Employers can't outlaw romance, regulate it or police it. However, workplaces must have rules or guidelines for when romance interferes with the fundamental purpose of the workplace – efficiency and effectiveness. What are the potential effects of having two of your team members romantic involved?

You may believe that as long as one person doesn't report to the other, there is no potential for conflict. Consider a couple that is unencumbered by other romantic or marital commitments, working in the same department, at the same level in the organization. They may be seen as a 'unit' by their colleagues or manager. Other team members or their team leader may be concerned that if negative feedback is given to one member of the couple, the other member will take that feedback personally. How would one member of the couple feel if the other was demoted, fired or laid off? If one half of the 'unit' was let go, and moved to another city for work, the organization may lose the second half of the 'unit' who may be a high performer.

If the relationship breaks up acrimoniously, the fallout could be severe. The other team members are likely to take sides, especially if they have known the two unit members for some time and have developed familial relationships. This could develop into two toxic work groups that find it impossible to work effectively together. The two employees involved could withhold information from each other or attempt to sabotage each other's work or career. If the relationship breaks up with one party remaining interested in the other and they pursue the of the relationship, that behaviour could be considered or could lead to harassment or stalking.

Possibilities of career and workplace damage increases if one 'unit' member reports to the other.

In the case of promotion where no other romantic entanglements are involved, consider the case of two information technologists who are romantically involved and work together as colleagues. After one year, the male is promoted to leader over a team of four others, including his romantic partner. This new dynamic is particularly conflict-ridden for the web of relationship has changed, not just between the couple, but all the relationships within the team.

The manager, in theory, would see his five team members equally. However, chances are none of his team members would perceive this fairness to exist.

His romantic partner would see that perhaps her partner must be tougher on her than the other three so that they don't see her being favoured. She would have to be prepared for her evaluations from her romantic partner to be seen as biased and tainted by her team members and senior management.

The other three team members would also be suspicious of any information they shared with their manager's partner. Does what they say to her go directly to him? Is venting a safe thing to do anymore? Can they give him feedback on her performance safely? Conversely, they may want to use her as an intermediary, even if she doesn't want to be involved or placed in an awkward situation.

In a more complicated situation, what if the relationship falls apart? The very public case of Dennis Carey and Marie-Caroline von Weichs shows what can happen when we don't think this possibility through.

Although in this case, the complainant is suing for wrongful dismissal, in every way it is a case of sexual harassment. Under the human rights codes across Canada, a case like this would be termed 'quid pro quo'. If a person is requested to provide some kind of sexual favour (from comments to intercourse) and they refuse to do so, and there is a negative impact on their job because of their refusal to do so, harassment has occurred.

In the dissolution of an affair between a manager and employee, conflict is rampant. Gossip and rumour floods through the organization, potential lawsuits exist, and productivity and morale plummet.

Idea #5 Clarify Clarify Clarify

The more diverse your team, the more communication is essential. Consider the following areas:

Goal: Has everyone been told the goal and how it will be measured? Ask each member: "What would success look like? How will we know when we achieve it?" You might think everyone is seeing the task or project the same, but asking them to verbalize it back to you will truly show any cracks in your communication.

Roles: Who will do what? Clarify who will do what and what won't they do. Follow the project flow as to who hands off what to whom and when. Particularly with language differences, different words mean different things. Is there agreement on time definitions such as "soon as possible"?

Rules: How are we going to play together? How will we deal with conflict, decision making, and disclosure to people outside the team? In some cultures, decisions are made by vote, others by consensus. Someone might think that you shouldn't bring errors to the attention of the person making them, someone else may think that this 'saving face' loses time and creates problems.

ENDNOTES

1. "Sex Lies and Lawsuits", *Fortune Magazine*, May 17, 2004, Peter Elkind.

CHAPTER SIXTEEN

Why Can We Do
As An Organization?

Organizations known for successfully promoting cultural diversity will attract the best and brightest candidates in the future. For example, organizations that have co-op programs or summer students and focus on diversity hiring, will have a higher likelihood of having these diverse temporary employees see their environment as preferable for permanent employment.

What kind of workplace do you have? What kind of organization do you want?

Here are ideas that may help your organization create a diversity-friendly environment.

Idea #1 Utilize diversity based analysis

Group based analysis is a tool to assist in systematically integrating diversity considerations into the policy planning and decision making processes. For example gender analysis considers how a decision affects men and women and diverse groups of men and women. Group based analysis is not advocacy or political correctness. It is a process that prevents unintended outcomes that might develop as a result of not considering all the groups in the organization.

For example, an organization may have a policy that states that all sales reps traveling on the road to a convention must share rooms. This policy might work if all the sales reps are of one gender, but what if there are uneven numbers of men and women?

Another example might be scheduling meetings without breaks. This could impact someone with health issues or someone with scheduled prayer times.

Idea #2 Create diversity skilled managers

The key skills needed to be a diversity skilled manager are the ability to give effective performance feedback, manage appropriate accommodation of differences, and to change leadership style to accommodate differences.

This requires more than a willingness on behalf of the manager, but effective diversity leadership training and support by the organization.

Idea #3 Utilize the diversity sitting dormant in your organization

Consider these examples:

I. A call centre serving clients across the US and Canada that has multi-lingual service reps has a distinct diversity advantage. If the organization streams calls to match the client with the service rep, they will have increased customer satisfaction.

II. If you struggle to get people to work days that many people consider to be holidays or are holidays by law (Christmas Day, Good Friday, and Thanksgiving weekend), consider utilizing those who are of faiths with high holidays at different times of the year. Create a system to 'switch' their time for a win/win outcome.

III. If you run 24/7, identify groups and appropriate matching shifts so staff are at their highest level of productivity. All employees value flexibility, but particularly night owls/early birds, people with parenting issues, elder issues, and religious requirements. Consider using a shift-scheduling specialist to identify your optimum shift schedule for highest effectiveness. Schedule training to match preferences as well.[1]

Idea #4 Bridge people into the culture

The more different someone is from the norm of the team, the more a mentor or coach is required. Consider a buddy system to coach new staff on your organization's culture and accommodate differences where possible.

Idea #5 Develop effective policies

Have clear policies for respectful workplace, bullying and harassment. Many people are confused by bullying and harassment and policies should be clear with definitions as how these two issues differ. Labor law, collective agreements, policies and human rights law should all dovetail to avoid confusion.

According to Heather Gray of TAMA Inc.,[2] workplace bullying is a phenomenon that is becoming increasingly recognized in many organizations as a serious management problem. Workplace bullying is the repeated, malicious verbal mistreatment of a target by a bully that is driven by the bully's desire to control the target (or what happens to the target).

Bullying is often confused with harassment, but there are distinct differences. It is the steady and yet very deliberate annihilation of an individual's self-esteem, career, reputation and sense of purpose and safety. Rarely do these situations fall under the protection and recourse of the human rights codes or other type of legislation. This is why separate policies must exist for harassment and bullying.

Do you have a harassment policy? Depending on whether you are federally or provincially legislated, you may be required by law to have a harassment or violence in the workplace policy.

Idea #6 Attach diversity initiatives to your performance management grid

Do you have a system in place to measure results, and do you hold the senior team and managers accountable for creating the diversity changes the organization desires? Do you hold managers responsible for turnover due to diverse employees leaving due to corporate 'miss-match'? Does performance management measure goals and objectives in the recruitment, development and retention of diversity groups?

Idea #7 Invest in training of staff on issues of respect, harassment and diversity

Idea #8 Have accountability frameworks

Does your organization:

- Make is easy for recruiters and managers to fall into the trap of hiring and promoting people who have the same cultural backgrounds as themselves? Do you have internal accountability frameworks in place for the recruitment and retention of diversity talent?

- Screen for and select suppliers that meet your standards for diversity?

- Have a zero-tolerance policy for racism and sexism?

- Have a policy that ensures quick response to harassment or discrimination complaints?

- Take a leadership role in helping under-represented groups overcome obstacles to their full inclusion in the labour market, such as:
- working with stakeholders to seek solutions regarding the recognition of foreign credentials
- helping newcomers to Canada gain valuable Canadian work experience
- funding community organizations that provide training in language and employment skills to immigrants?

ENDNOTES

1. For shift schedules, see *www.alertatwork.com*.

2. For more information about TAMA Inc (Threat Assessment and Management Associates, Inc.) see *www.tamainc.net*.

CHAPTER SEVENTEEN
Why Should We Care?

Ernest H. Drew, CEO of Hoechst Celanese described a singular event as the defining moment that converted him to an advocate for diversity. It occurred at a retreat for his 125 senior people who were mostly white males and 50 lower level employees who were mostly women and visible minorities. Part way through the retreat, the attendees split up into small teams to discuss issues dealing with corporate culture and productivity. Some teams were diverse, others predominately white male.

Drew said that when the teams presented their findings, *"It was so obvious that the diverse teams had the broader solutions. They had ideas I'd never thought of. For the first time, we realized that diversity is a strength as it relates to problem solving. Before we thought of diversity as the total number of minorities and women in the company...now we know we needed diversity at every level of the company where decisions are made."*[1]

If excellence requires the best use of resources, then an inclusive and representative workforce is one key to economic success. Many employers recognize the business advantages of diversity in the workforce: better customer service, a broader range of job applicants, enrichment of workplace culture, and the creative energy generated by a variety of perspectives.

Until we see the value of diversity with our own eyes, however, it is sometimes difficult to embrace this concept. In teams, we can see the value of diversity in something as simple as a crossword puzzle. But for real change in an organization, commitment must come from the top and flow down, with the senior executive's beliefs about a diverse work force vocal and emphatic.

ENDNOTES

1. "How to Make Diversity Pay", *Fortune Magazine*, August 1994.

INDEX

About the Author

Jeanne Martinson is a professional speaker, trainer and best selling author who has worked throughout Canada and internationally. Since starting her own firm in 1993, Jeanne has inspired thousands of participants in her workshops and keynote presentations with her humour, insight and real-world examples.

As Managing Partner of her own firm, Martrain Corporate and Personal Development, Jeanne has worked with corporations, government and non-profit organizations, developing and delivering keynotes and workshops in the areas of leadership and diversity.

When not delivering workshops or keynotes, Jeanne is very active in her community. Her contributions have been recognized with the Canada 125 Medal of Honour, the YWCA Woman of Distinction Award in the category of Business, Labour and Professions, the Canadian Federation of Business and Professional Women's "Outstanding Woman of the Year" Award, the Saskatchewan Centennial Leadership Medal, and listings in Canadian Who's Who directories.

PUBLICATIONS BY JEANNE MARTINSON

War and Peace in the Workplace:
Diversity – Conflict – Understanding – Reconciliation
Ever wonder why we can't just get along? Why we react to each other
the way we do? Most conflict in the workplace comes from our
differences - both our diversity in the big 'D' issues such as race,
gender, or ability but also diversity in the small 'd' issues such as
values, marital and family status, age or thought processes. Diversity
can be problematic and it can be wonderful. As individuals and
organizations, we can benefit from the many perspectives that create
the synergy to move an organization forward by leaps and bounds.
On the other hand, differences can trigger conflict, toxic work groups,
low morale, harassment, misunderstandings and employee turnover.
Many organizations adopt respectful workplace or harassment
policies. But this isn't enough to realize the benefits of a diverse
workforce or to minimize diversity based conflict. We need to shift
how we perceive and work with others. This book illustrates how we
have the choice between allowing conflict to spiral down into
dysfunction or of taking charge, becoming aware and developing
understanding. It's all up to us!

Escape from Oz – Leadership in the 21st Century explores the
parallels of the characters in the fable The Wonderful Wizard of Oz
and our own beliefs about personal and professional leadership. The
first part of the book explores the four cornerstones required to be
effective leaders and the second part of the book explores how we can
move out of our comfort zone to lead individuals according to their
reality, skill set and knowledge base – with the goal of achieving trust
and long term success. This book about the basics of personal
leadership and leading others, is written to assist you in becoming an
effective leader - whether you are leading a committee of one or a
corporation of five thousand.

Lies and Fairy Tales That Deny Women Happiness explores why
women think the way the do – and why they sometimes bungle their
professional and personal relationships. It looks at the fairy tales
women grow up with (Cinderella, Snow White, Beauty and the Beast,
and Sleeping Beauty) and analyzes how the beliefs that women hold
on to from these stories can affect their ability to be successful.

All available at www.martrain.org

About Martrain

Corporate Seminars and Workshops

An organization's greatest asset is its people. Our workshop solutions assist you in releasing your organization's hidden excellence.

Leading a Diverse Workplace

Leadership for the 21st Century

Diversity and Respect in the Workplace

Preventing Harassment in the Workplace

Keynote Presentations

Conferences and special events are remembered because of their speakers and presenters. Jeanne combines humour, real life experience, and quality information to educate and entertain your conference participants.

The Co-Dependent Leader

Leadership for the 21st Century

Keeping Trust: The Glue of Leadership

Thriving in a Changing Workplace:
Learning to Behave out of the Ordinary

Diversity: What Does it Mean to My Business?

Leadership Audits

Do you have a department or branch that doesn't seem to be working but you can't figure out why? A Leadership Audit may help. A Leadership Audit involves interviews with staff (new, old, and gone) and their leader to determine leadership issues that need to be addressed.

CONTACT INFO

All correspondence, as well as requests for seminars and speaking engagements should be forwarded to:

Martrain Corporation and Personal Development
P.O. Box 1216
Regina, Saskatchewan
Canada S4P 3B4
www.martrain.org
email: watertiger@sasktel.net
Tel: 306.569.0388
Fax: 306.569.0302

ORDER FORMS

ORDER FORM

I wish to order additional copies of:

Quantity

War & Peace In the Workplace   _____

Escape From Oz–Leadership for the 21st Century   _____

Lies & Fairy Tales That Deny Women Happiness   _____

Name: _____

Shipping Address: _____

City: _____ Prov. ____ Postal Code_____

$22.00 each (Canadian) or $20.00 (US)
plus $2.00 for tax, shipping & handling

Please make payment by cheque to:
Martrain
P.O. Box 1216
Regina, SK Canada S4P 3B4

ORDER FORM

I wish to order additional copies of:

Quantity

War & Peace In the Workplace   _____

Escape From Oz–Leadership for the 21st Century   _____

Lies & Fairy Tales That Deny Women Happiness   _____

Name: _____

Shipping Address: _____

City: _____ Prov. ____ Postal Code_____

$22.00 each (Canadian) or $20.00 (US)
plus $2.00 for tax, shipping & handling

Please make payment by cheque to:
Martrain
P.O. Box 1216
Regina, SK Canada S4P 3B4